7~~00~~
Inspiring Guides
to a
New Life

Vernon Howard

New Life Foundation
www.anewlife.org

New Life Foundation
PO Box 2230
Pine AZ 85544

ISBN 0-911203-42-7

How This Book Serves You

For personal progress: The guides in this book contain dynamic principles for revealing a totally new world to you. Some guides supply unique information, while others awaken fresh inspiration.

Each is a complete and independent contributor to daily enrichment. You will read many fascinating stories about men and women who are winning the same special success you wish to find. Choose whichever path you prefer for the day: 1. Start with any numbered guide and read for awhile. 2. Select and benefit from one of the *Practical Reading Programs.*

For speakers and teachers: The 700 guides can be used to illustrate points in your lecture and to make the message clearer and more attractive in general. Each guide contains a story or description, a simile, a word-picture or some other feature which makes a message sparkle. Use them freely. Here are four ways to use the book when conducting classes:

1. Read a guide aloud and lead the group in a discussion of its outstanding points.

2. Ask students to mention the most helpful idea each gained from a reading.

3. Invite questions from those who wish more light on a subject.

4. Request volunteers to read at home a guide of their choice and bring a short report on it to class.

Remember, your real nature becomes new every moment. So now walk forward toward the ever-present dawn until becoming one with it, for in this oneness is a quiet command of all of life.

—Vernon Howard

Practical Reading Programs

Here are twenty-five reading programs which contain an abundance of answers and satisfactions. Simply read the guides in the arranged order, pondering and absorbing as you proceed.

Program 1: 15, 52, 131, 157, 204, 244, 283, 335, 381, 432, 485, 555, 579, 636, 696.

Program 2: 23, 78, 127, 163, 227, 281, 320, 358, 414, 453, 510, 528, 595, 613, 662.

Program 3: 39, 65, 98, 155, 200, 247, 301, 350, 392, 462, 504, 547, 608, 640, 683.

Program 4: 41, 93, 134, 165, 212, 259, 288, 333, 423, 440, 475, 564, 587, 623, 700.

Program 5: 17, 49, 107, 158, 195, 274, 302, 360, 409, 457, 511, 533, 594, 638, 672.

Program 6: 45, 87, 141, 181, 221, 262, 292, 356, 403, 448, 482, 521, 606, 643, 693.

Program 7: 31, 59, 122, 171, 235, 267, 325, 343, 382, 461, 505, 563, 576, 651, 688.

Program 8: 42, 68, 109, 147, 210, 243, 291, 376, 394, 435, 474, 560, 567, 625, 676.

Program 9: 2, 74, 126, 182, 217, 256, 323, 359, 412, 452, 514, 539, 610, 639, 675.

Program 10: 6, 75, 123, 150, 193, 278, 299, 372, 385, 427, 506, 556, 571, 615, 666.

Program 11: 29, 67, 100, 162, 224, 265, 306, 337, 401, 443, 500, 558, 611, 648, 697.

Program 12: 18, 90, 113, 156, 190, 253, 317, 366, 387, 438, 471, 531, 600, 646, 663.

Program 13: 9, 60, 132, 175, 232, 277, 315, 374, 422, 467, 517, 561, 598, 650, 691.

Program 14: 37, 62, 140, 172, 219, 264, 305, 342, 380, 433, 498, 548, 609, 637, 677.

Program 15: 3, 54, 103, 146, 197, 257, 328, 373, 402, 441, 502, 522, 573, 656, 669.

Program 16: 1, 56, 118, 145, 226, 271, 289, 362, 405, 428, 479, 553, 589, 617, 698.

Program 17: 12, 63, 108, 166, 229, 248, 297, 341, 388, 444, 491, 540, 607, 642, 659.

Program 18: 46, 82, 115, 185, 208, 269, 309, 361, 396, 456, 490, 523, 581, 628, 661.

Program 19: 27, 88, 139, 174, 214, 245, 295, 348, 413, 469, 509, 545, 602, 616, 670.

Program 20: 5, 72, 136, 170, 223, 272, 312, 364, 398, 437, 480, 525, 575, 649, 686.

Program 21: 28, 70, 101, 188, 218, 239, 296, 345, 384, 451, 497, 535, 566, 653, 680.

Program 22: 14, 80, 137, 160, 233, 250, 322, 371, 420, 449, 492, 546, 592, 645, 673.

Program 23: 34, 50, 104, 169, 201, 258, 308, 339, 418, 436, 501, 552, 585, 627, 660.

Program 24: 21, 66, 133, 178, 199, 273, 284, 370, 407, 459, 472, 536, 569, 620, 679.

Program 25: 8, 55, 110, 144, 205, 246, 310, 346, 393, 430, 477, 551, 604, 632, 685.

Contents

POWER AND PLEASURE IN HUMAN RELATIONS

1. There was once a strange land where everyone walked backward. Boys and girls born there were taught that the backward walk was the normal walk, which they accepted without question. Since no one could see where he was going, spills and collisions became a miserable way of life. But here is the strangest part of the story. Rarely did anyone reflect, "But this feels so awkward. Could there be a *natural* way to walk?" There is, and you can find it.

2. "My vague dread for many years," a student admitted, "was that I would repeat the same mistakes, that I would do again what I did before. But one explanation in this class brightened everything. I now see how conscious behavior can break mechanical behavior. I feel less tense about everything." Another student nodded and added, "Rightness releases relief."

3. Most people wander puzzledly through life, like small children in a museum. They simply do not know how to do good to themselves. So do you know why you should think about these celestial principles? Because every time you do it does you good. Now, what better reason could you have? *It does you good.*

4. "To test your attentiveness to tonight's main lesson," a teacher told his class, "I will ask you a question. Suppose a distressed man asks you why he continues to experience one difficulty after another, both inwardly and outwardly. How would you answer?" A student responded, "I would tell him it is because he still prefers to play society's foolish game in the hope of winning a reward—which will be an attractive but empty box. The alternative is for him to make a place in himself for corrective facts, which will surely arrive."

11

5. You can learn to conquer fear because you can learn how to be nonexistent to fear. It is like removing a target so that an arrow has nothing to penetrate. Explained briefly, you remove yourself as a target by seeing that you are not the self made by society's descriptions, but consist of a Universal Self.

6. A new class was told, "In this group we don't care about your past. We care about your present. And that is all that must concern you. Be attentive to what you can do for yourself right now. This should make you as eager as a child at a picnic. I will give you a hint of good things to come. You will no longer fear what you now fear so deeply that you are afraid to even mention it to anyone. You will be fearless, bold, victorious."

7. William Herschel was born in Hanover, Germany, in 1738, the son of a musician. Though an acclaimed musician himself, Herschel had a secret love—astronomy. He constructed his own telescopes which enabled him to see starry wonders never before seen by man. So great was his love for higher worlds that he used to slip into a back room between concert selections to gaze upward for a few minutes. He eventually discovered the planet Uranus. We must also have a love for higher worlds. It will certainly lead to great cosmic discoveries.

8. People find it hard to believe that Truth exists on earth for those who really want it. Truth seems so out of place in this desperate world, like a book of poems on a battlefield. People cannot see Truth because of misplaced attention. They attend to the social battle because they wrongly think they must be winners. But the battle really exists only in their misused minds, which Truth wants them to see. The seeing is the healing.

9. A speaker told his audience, "When I see your sad and weary faces I know something about you. I know you are under a hypnotic spell. But I also know that you do not know you are under this unnecessary spell. You *are* the spell, so you are unable to see it. My task is to make you see that a spell is only a spell. How many times have I told you to wake up? I will tell you again. Wake up!"

10. Truth's strength does not depend upon your belief or lack of belief in it. You can be very grateful for that. Truth's power is as independent of human thought as sunlight is independent of the wind. To understand this, blend with Truth.

11. A story written in Finland told of a brickmaker who was hauling his products to market on a dark night. He complained bitterly at the bumpy road he and his wagon had to travel. Then he noticed something. He was making his own rough road by carelessly permitting the bricks to fall off the wagon and under the wheels. Because men and women travel at night—in mental darkness—they fail to see how they make their own rough roads. Correction is possible.

12. Real encouragement can come only from an awakened man who does not see people as they see themselves. True encouragement occurred in a class when a teacher stated, "I do not see you as permanently chained by time. I see you as individuals who can be free of regrets toward the past and free of anxieties toward the future." What could be more encouraging?

13. No doctor can cure a sick man who insists he is healthy. The patient must become honest about his actual condition, which permits the cure. Truth cannot

heal anyone who denies the need for healing. But a surface admission of illness is not enough. The patient must submit to a spiritual X-ray, must permit truth to see what he is really like. This is not dangerous, as the patient may imagine, but is the start of a marvelous and permanent healing. It only makes sense to start right now.

14. Authentic self-change is the result of acquiring fresh insights. This change can be clearly observed in those who earnestly seek fresh insights. An example of this occurred when one student stood up in class. "I now see," he stated, "how my own cravings attracted certain people and conditions into my life. I see myself as the cause of my experiences. My present aim is to change myself in order to change what happens to me."

15. Everyone has enough wisdom to *begin* self-study. Everyone has enough energy to *start* self-transformation. So just begin. You will then find fresh wisdom and energy for each new beginning. One man made an excellent start by remembering that he was a part of the universe, therefore, universal forces were his very own forces.

16. "Be your own teacher," some students were instructed. "For example, teach yourself that your real nature is alive but asleep, like a tree in winter. You can invite springtime any time you like. Teach that to yourself. And be a good pupil."

17. At a certain point along the path a definite realization appears. You see that all your weaknesses and anxieties were caused by your immersion in

psychic sleep. Now you do not blame yourself for wrong past behavior, but at the same time you never excuse yourself. This blending of two understandings develops power for self-awakening, just as wind and sail combine to move a boat. Weakness and anxiety toward people will disappear.

18. "It might help someone," a student remarked in class, "if I mention a self-defeating habit I used to have. Whenever truth offered its correction I would disappear, either physically or psychologically. By psychological disappearance I mean I would run away into my usual ego-protecting attitudes or into fearful scorn of the person trying to help me. If any of you are still doing that, stop it for your own sake."

19. Suppose two people read the same truthful book or attend the same inspiring lecture. Because one of them can no longer endure his pretense, he gains something. Because the other cannot bear to be seen through, he gains nothing. The difference in the two is the difference between a solid door which blocks light and a glass door which admits light. Open your mind to the healing light.

20. Some visitors to Colorado pulled their car off the road to check their location. A few miles ahead they saw a small town. Needing food and supplies, they drove to the village—to discover that it was not what it appeared to be. It was an empty village, set up for making a movie. In life, we mistake the illusory for the real, then wonder why our needs are not supplied.

DISCOVER THE SECRET OF THE AGES

21. An authentic teaching makes sense only when it is recognized by the authentic *you*. Discover the nature of this authentic *you* and the secret of the ages is yours. The *you* is what remains when all self-descriptions and all of society's labels about you have been removed. To really know what is inside a package you must ignore its advertising and examine its contents personally. Self-examination reveals the authentic *you* which instantly recognizes an authentic message — the only message making sense here on earth.

22. Every difficulty contains its own solution, just as a guiding star is especially bright on a dark night. Do you ever feel that others have cruel power over you? It is a fact that no one has dominating power unless your own fear gives him that power. So investigate why you have this fear, and your findings will make the fear a thing of the past.

23. Results arise according to natural laws, but arrogant men claim that results come from their personal skill and wisdom. Fearing to lose his wealth to thieves, a man buried a bag of gold in a large field. To mark the spot he noticed a cloud directly overhead. A year later he returned to the field, noticed an overhead cloud, dug into the earth and recovered his gold. "How clever of me," he congratulated himself, "for marking the spot like that."

24. A desperate man asked a friend to recommend a source of help. The friend responded, "I know a man who is good and wise in the highest meanings of those words. He understands the mysteries of man and the universe. He has no artificial manners, no need to get

anything from those who seek him out. He is a source of authentic help." The desperate man interrupted impatiently, "Please get to the point. How many years did he attend college?"

25. A movie maker set out alone into rugged country to take films of beavers. Falling ill, he could see no way of attracting help. Then he thought of a plan. He attached his camera to a raft which was then permitted to float downstream. Raft and camera were sighted by alert park rangers who quickly developed the film, thus learning the location of the movie maker who was soon rescued. Likewise, part of you knows how to attract right help. Let it do so. Release rich resources.

26. A general was leading his army on a march through a Dutch town. The philosopher Baruch Spinoza lived in that town. Having been impressed with the teachings of Spinoza, the general halted his march in order to talk with the Dutch philosopher. Men and women must halt their thoughtless march through life to listen to something higher than themselves.

27. An office worker returned to the building one night to obtain some files. He was annoyed to find that the key given to him did not fit the lock. He mentally blamed the office manager for giving him the wrong key. Then, to his chagrin, he realized he had mixed up the right key with some of his home keys. Man is always trying to solve the puzzle of his life, rarely realizing that he himself is the only puzzle he has. The puzzle can be solved.

28. Make a simple declaration and go into action with it. You might state, "People and circumstances do not have power to upset me." This is a fact on the cosmic

level, so you must now uplift your mind to this higher level to make it a personal experience. Go beyond the words to the experience, just as you set aside the menu to possess the actual dinner.

29. "It may help," said a student to the class, "if I pass on to you some advice that helped me in the earlier days. Here it is. Do not let people occupy your time with their foolish chatter and their complicated theories about life. Toss out everything except your aim to be a clear-minded man or woman."

30. An individual receives according to his requests. If receiving strife and misfortune they come because of his personal request. He finds this difficult to accept, but it is still a fact, and one he must grasp. A man's negative nature asks for strife, but since he is unaware of this actual nature he cannot see the connection between asking and receiving. A hawk's nature asks for other hawks, but a dove attracts other doves.

31. Thoughts cannot rise above their own level any more than a lake can raise its level by its own effort. This explains why individuals and nations are unable to correct destructive behavior. They attempt the impossible task of using the conditioned mind to correct the conditioned mind, which is like washing clothes in muddy water. The only corrective action is that unique power we can call by any name we choose, such as God, Cosmic Consciousness, Inner Kingdom. Seek only this supreme solution to personal problems.

32. A teacher explained to a class, "People believe they defend what is true and right when in fact they cunningly defend their own personal interests in what they call right. This personal interest can never be right,

for what is right for one must be wrong for another. True rightness is above crafty personal interest and therefore needs no defender."

33. Some scholars were given many attractive medals in recognition of their profound wisdom. They were then commissioned to carry their knowledge to the natives of a distant and uncivilized land. When their ship was caught in a storm the captain shouted, "We must lighten the load! Toss overboard whatever you value the least!" The scholars kept the medals and tossed their books overboard. Not all scholars are wise.

34. Cosmic Intelligence alone can create human harmony, for Cosmic Intelligence exists in the absence of human egotism and rivalry. It is artificial intelligence which divides man against man, as when two smiling schemers turn sour when seeing through each other. Cosmic Intelligence creates undivided illumination, just as ten candles fill the room with one light.

35. A student entered a room where a teacher was counseling a new arrival at the school. The student won something he needed by hearing the teacher tell the newcomer, "Just ask whether or not you make sense to yourself. Answer with bold honesty. This opens the door to a life of superior sense. To repeat, ask whether you make sense to yourself. If not, make correction."

36. Why does a flooding river carry away a house on the riverbank? Because the house was foolishly built on the riverbank. Why is a man carried away by worldly floods of violence and sorrow? Because he foolishly builds his psychic house on society's riverbank. Fortunately, he can move to high ground.

37. In a class in San Francisco the teacher asked everyone to contribute a short and helpful thought. One student offered, "When you take an uncomfortable situation as an inner exercise, rather than with the annoyance felt by most people, you already have something unusual." Use *everything* for inner-development.

38. People wonder what an illuminated man would tell them if they were to meet. Suppose you asked such a truly intelligent man, "What do I need to know for the sake of my own happiness?" Among his advices would be the teaching, "The wrong way appears to be the easy way, but it is still the hard way. The right way appears to be the hard way, but it is still the easy way."

39. There is one great moment when a man begins to win something worth winning. It is the moment when the exterior battle turns into internal conflict. The fact is, the battle was inside all the time, but for the first time he sees the actual location of both the bombs and the resulting wounds. Now, like a soldier who has learned the enemy's secrets, he knows how to win.

40. A pharmacist amused the rest of the group by relating, "I now see the difference between the classes I used to attend and this class. In the other classes I suspected that the teacher saw through me. In this class I *know* he does!"

HOW UNUSUAL DELIGHT APPEARS

41. A certain Arabian tribe used to consider it shameful for anyone to ride a camel, for horses only were held in respect. But one tribesman, lost in the sandy hills, rode a camel to safety. He was surprised at feeling no shame, feeling only a delight at saving himself.

Any strangeness felt when first using new and unfamiliar facts will soon fade, to be replaced by unusual delight.

42. Imagine yourself on vacation. While driving the highway you pause at interesting sights along the way, perhaps a monument or a historical town. You do not want to miss anything. Be equally interested in every pause along the inward journey. Do not dismiss a lesson as trivial or as something already familiar. Peer intently at each lesson as if it has a secret message for you, which it does. Practice with this lesson: Pearls will come to you once you cease to believe that pebbles are pearls.

43. A man felt he had sunk too deeply into foolish ways to ever return to a sensible life. He stated this belief to a teacher, after which the teacher instructed, "Drop your ring into the dust." Removing his valuable ring, the man dropped it to the ground. "See?" the teacher concluded the lesson. "The ring is still valuable." Anyone who wishes to come back home can come back home.

44. Never believe society when it claims to love individual independence. Society is on the side of individuality as much as the wolf is on the side of the lamb. Only a real individual champions the cause of individuality. Listen to such a man.

45. Courage must be defined from a spiritual viewpoint, not from man's shallow words and standards. Courage is the willingness to continue to listen to blunt facts about oneself while realizing that these facts may make drastic inner changes necessary. These arousing facts may come from another person or from one's own dim light which is trying to become a bright light.

One man showed true courage by realizing that he knew far fewer answers to life than he pretended to know. Abundant answers came to that man.

46. Like a spring spreading its waters uselessly into desert sands, man wastes inner powers which could be channeled toward creativity and refreshment. Today, decide to use your powers for inner advancement. Have you ever wished for freedom from the harmful influences of other people? That wish is a definite power. Let it guide you all the way to self-independence.

47. When a married couple inquired of a teacher, the husband said, "You have observed us in class for many weeks. What personal advice do we need?" The teacher replied, "People often criticize themselves in front of others to soften the pain of anticipated criticism from others. I have noticed this in both of you. End it. If criticized, take the full blow consciously, remembering everything you have learned in class. You will grow."

48. Man is always anxious because he knows he cannot confidently carry his assumed self into every situation. He is like an actor suddenly onstage with a role he has not rehearsed. The confident businessman finds himself wordless when his aged parents ask him about eternity. The socially active woman feels depressed when confined in bed with illness. But whoever lives from his Whole Self goes anywhere with perfect ease.

49. An assistant at an esoteric school welcomed a group of new pupils and then gave them the following explanation. "A real teacher is gentle in order to give people just as much truth as they can take at a time. A false teacher is gentle because he fears his audience. A real teacher is stern in order to arouse people to

cosmic awakening. A false teacher is stern because there is something wrong with him." The new pupils understood.

50. Others may neglect the offered guiding lights, but we will be wiser. We want to know what can be known, we want to reach what it is possible to possess. So let your spiritual enthusiasm be like a thirsty root which eagerly stretches out for more and more water. Your reward is certain.

51. One sly way in which egotism hangs onto itself is by superficial admissions of weakness or bewilderment. But the person's manner reveals subtle boasting and vanity. He is the center of attention; also, he hopes to impress others with his humility. His confession is as false as a cannon covered with roses. This is just another unconscious self-trick which must go if the individual is to grow. Self-growth is a great law of life.

52. If only you will realize the great number of things you need *not* think about. What a relief! You need not anxiously think about being liked or disliked by others, for neither attitude connects with the real you. You need not strain to think of ways to become more intelligent, for true discernment blossoms by itself as fantasies fade. Because a child's immature mind creates the idea of a ghost he must then worriedly wonder how to escape it. But an adult's mature mind has nothing to think about.

53. A boy's rubber ball accidentally flew over a high wall into a neighbor's yard. Every few minutes the boy approached the wall to call out, "I want my ball back." After one such request an unseen hand threw the ball

back to the persistent boy. Approach your invisible nature within to declare, "I want my life back." It will be given you.

54. When someone falls into trouble he is always surprised. That is like being surprised to find Spaniards in Spain. He is shocked that the mind he calls logical could have dragged him into the marsh. The question is, what else on earth did he expect a confused mind to drag him into? A clear mind supplies a pleasant day.

55. People living in self-contradiction never know which way to turn when troubled. Separated from the Supreme Source, they turn anxiously to substitutes, such as seeking agreement from others that they have been cruelly wronged. That is the repeated and the pathetic story of their lives. The single-minded person is different. Like a tree growing by a stream, he has a sure source of strength—a Supreme Source.

56. Make your own life-map and you will know it is accurate. A king who had just ascended the throne wanted to know the nature of his kingdom. He asked his ten governors to send him maps of their regions, which they did. But when the king visited the regions the maps turned out to be incorrect. Lakes were pictured where deserts existed. Roads were shown to run north and south but actually ran east and west. Tossing out the maps, the king explored the kingdom for himself, after which he ruled with ease and efficiency.

57. A disciple praised an Eastern wise man, "Great teacher, you have renounced wealth and fame for the sake of truth. How noble a sacrifice!" The wise man replied, "How little you understand. Does a man sacrifice anything by giving up childish toys in exchange for a cosmic empire?"

58. How does inner change—real and lasting change—make our actions truly beneficial? Remember the nature of real change. It consists of additional illumination of a new and bright understanding of why we act as we do. It is this illumination which steers us into beneficial actions, just as a miner knows what to do after switching on his light.

59. The weaker the man the more he believes himself strong. This belief, this illusion, punishes him in several ways. It forces him to fawn before those who agree to agree with his illusion—for a price. He must burden himself with tense defense, like a knight weighted down with heavy and uncomfortable armor. But worst of all, he cuts himself off from the truly strong who could show him how to be truly strong himself.

60. A teacher sent a thrill of true inspiration through his listeners by saying, "I do not accept sullen submission as a way of life for myself and I do not accept it for you. Stop accepting resentful submission as necessary and you will find it unnecessary. But remember, I am not advocating rebellion against anything but your own psychic hypnosis. I accept liberty alone for you. Accept liberty alone for yourself."

SOLVING THE MYSTERY OF SUFFERING

61. The reason for humanity's destructive psychic hypnosis is no mystery. An individual cannot be told what he must be told. As hard as ice, he refuses to be melted by Truth. Think of anyone you know. Imagine someone bluntly asking him or her, "Why do you pretend to know what you are doing with your life when part of you senses it is all a nervous bluff?" You can

also imagine the resentful response. So the mystery of humanity's endless suffering is solved.

62. Navigation of the cosmic ship requires a captain and a crew. But the captain must take charge of the crew, not permitting it to create chaos by running wildly all over the ship. The crew consists of thousands of thoughts which must be trained to serve, not damage. The captain consists of a point of consciousness within the man. This captain knows the cosmic harbor he wants to reach.

63. Stated a new student, "I have lived in false confidence over the years. I feel confident as long as things are going my way, but the smallest challenge can shake me." Commented the teacher, "Real confidence is the absence of all thought about confidence, just as light is the absence of darkness. As long as you think about confidence you must also worry over nonconfidence, for both occupy the same plane of thought. In this class you will learn to rise above ordinary thought, which provides effortless confidence."

64. A story by a Swiss writer told about a man whose possessions had been carried away and scattered by a flood. The man patiently spent an entire year recovering his property. Our task is similar. We must recover our scattered psychic possessions, including self-awareness and self-energy.

65. Remember why you are here on earth. You are in this world for an opportunity to rise above the mechanical level of existence to become a conscious human being. Stated differently, you are here to unite yourself with the Cosmic Whole. When asked why he had dedicated his life to this aim, a student replied,

"What else is worthwhile?" Make the same noble reply for yourself.

66. It is easy for your true nature to be strong at all times in every circumstance. Our artificial nature cannot believe this because it has never experienced this effortless strength. A rabbit cannot understand the power of a horse. But real strength, cosmic strength, exists in fact. It is earned by those who are tired of being frightened children, by those who yearn for cosmic adulthood. This new strength enables you to enjoy people.

67. A party of scientists wished to climb a pinnacle in the mountains with the aim of establishing a weather station. But the pinnacle's steep and rocky sides appeared to make the ascent impossible. But an exploration of the pinnacle's base revealed a natural tunnel which led to a cavern inside. Another natural tunnel led from the cavern to the top of the pinnacle. A man's efforts to reach high ground are frustrated only because of his neglect of the natural way. The natural way opens before daring explorers.

68. Just as you might open the door to a room full of treasure, you can open a new door in your mind. Your treasure consists of knowledge of what you are all about and what your life is all about. How much are you worth? You are worth as much as you know about yourself. Collect self-knowledge!

69. Ten men and women sought to enroll in an esoteric school. The teacher asked them, "What have you brought with you?" One said he had brought considerable money, another said she had brought her fame, a third said he possessed power and influence.

The last man confessed, "I have brought the only thing I really have—a concealed bundle of hostilities and deceits." Exclaimed the teacher, "Ah! That is what the others have, too, but are unaware of it. You are accepted."

70. A piano needs only to be in tune with itself to provide pleasant music. You need only be in tune with yourself to provide your own pleasant life. Discover what this means. Here is a start: To be in tune means to no longer live from senseless ideas passed on to you by those whose own lives were empty. Be in tune with yourself by dropping the false guide of "I have been told."

71. In the early days of railroads in Africa an odd event occurred. An engineer connected his locomotive to a string of boxcars which he believed contained lumber. However, the boxcars actually contained a shipment of wild animals, which were carried to a large city. Fortunately, the error was discovered before the boxcars were opened. Man wrongly connects himself with wild emotions, which must be understood and turned into harmless feelings. Truth itself will help you climb to this higher level.

72. Said someone in class to the teacher, "I just want to thank you for not letting us take the easy way out. All of us much prefer to hide things from ourselves, which you did not permit. You insisted upon honest self-facing. Even when resisting the lesson we know of its necessity. So thank you. That's all."

73. Our sadness is both false and ridiculous. We are sad because we are not the success or the power or the attraction we falsely think we must become. You need not become anything except yourself, which calls for

an investigation of your unseen nature. Man is a king who sleeps and dreams he must become a king!

74. Truth never condemns anyone for anything. It simply informs everyone that he lives unknowingly in a state of psychic hypnosis which attracts all his griefs. Truth cordially invites everyone to listen to the necessary instructions for self-awakening. Truth teaches, "See your need for facing an entirely new direction. Remember, when facing the sun, the shadow is at your back."

75. Quite often a single sentence from a book or speaker can mark the turning point in a life. One woman heard the following in a lecture: "Notice how unhappy people are with their sources of happiness, how insecure they are with their securities." It helped her see the shallowness of her life, which turned her toward the light at last. The light can also be yours.

76. Like a warship disguised as a fishing vessel, man is not what he appears to be. So when in daily contacts with people, remember the law of opposites. The more someone prides himself on independent thinking, the less his ability to reason freely. The more he tries to convince you of his sincere intentions, the less trustworthy his nature. The more lavish the care on the exterior, the less value on the interior. Never forget these facts.

77. An awakened man remains in invisible command of his circumstances, even though it may appear to others that he is commanded by them. Having conquered deceitful desire, having no need to prove himself, his command consists of simply not fighting psychological circumstances. An ordinary man fights because his illusory self feels threatened by conditions. The

enlightened man has only a Universal Self which cannot be threatened by anything. He is a successful mountain climber who has escaped the floods in the valley below. This can be you.

78. Place a new value on *understanding*. Make understanding your great goal in life. Start by seeing how little you presently understand about your life here on earth. That is true humility which fills the cup with understanding. The amount of water in a cup is determined by the size of the cup, and you can make the cosmic cup just as large as you wish. What an opportunity!

79. A class in Delaware tried to see how egotism produced sorrow and darkness. One student contributed, "The connection between egotism and sadness can be illustrated. The larger the tree the greater the shadow."

80. Only a free man can live life on his own terms, which are the terms of his own real nature. All others live under unconscious and arrogant dictatorship. They are told what to do by interior compulsions and exterior influences. Having no life of their own, they are forced to change their manners with painful frequency, just as clothing changes under the dictates of fashion. Become a free man, a free woman.

A STORY ABOUT STRANGE HUMANITY

81. A lazy frog climbed upon a log in a pond to take a nap. A second lazy frog joined him, then others until twelve lazy frogs were dozing on the log. Unable to bear the weight, the log sank and rolled, spilling the twelve frogs into the pond. The spluttering frogs

assembled on the bank to declare, "We must find the guilty criminal who caused us to sink!" Sighting an energetic frog who was building a home, the lazy frogs cried out, "He must be the guilty one! Notice how he avoids the company of energetic and respectable frogs like us!"

82. The more usual an individual is the more he flatters himself on being unusual. Thinking of himself as unusual is what makes him usual. The most usual thing on earth is to be neurotic. A teacher overheard one disciple say to another, "I wish to achieve something truly different." The teacher approached to compliment, "Splendid! Become a healthy-minded human being."

83. Imagine yourself watching an artist painting an outdoor scene. You watch with interest as he develops the painting. There is one thing you do not do. You do not judge the painting by the first few strokes, that is, you do not imagine what the final picture will be like. You suspend judgment until seeing the whole picture. Inwardly, proceed as wisely. Suspend judgment so that the skillful artist within can present you with the complete and satisfying picture of your life.

84. Some men and women visited a teacher. Their spokesman said to him, "We think the right start is to ask ourselves what we would be like if we possessed love and understanding." Replied the teacher, "No, no. The right start is to ask yourselves what you would be like if all your masks were taken away."

85. Look at your hand. It is true right now that your hand is capable of performing hundreds of useful actions. You need not wait an hour or a day for its service, for it is always ready right now. Now look

inwardly. Whatever is inwardly true is true right now. This means you have power right now to cast out everything unwanted. So postpone no more. Act. You can now discover the pearl in the depths of your psychic sea.

86. I will show you what to do the next time you do not know what to do about a problem. Ask yourself, "What would I do if there were no *me* to either promote or protect?" Ask this over and over, even though not understanding its meaning. A sensing of its hidden power will arrive. In relief, inner clouds will turn to clear skies, and problems with people will vanish.

87. In your quest of self-command you will eventually attain a remarkable talent. You will be able to cut off a negative thought before it penetrates your psychic system to do damage. Being very alert, you cut it off at once, just as the conductor of an orchestra cuts off disharmony with a single wave of his baton.

88. Part of a teacher's talk in a class in Pennsylvania went like this: "No true idea can ever be in conflict with whatever is true within you. Any true idea is always in perfect harmony with whatever is true in you. When conflict exists it is because a true part within you has been set aside in favor of an untrue part within you or within another person to whom you are listening."

89. One night a young woman was offered employment in a beautiful country estate. However, she had to leave at once, which meant she had to stay awake in order to make the journey. Her wish for the attractive position kept her awake all the way. Let your wish for a new life keep you inwardly awake.

90. A man who saw deeply into human nature revealed four facts about people. "To see where a man is weak, listen to his boast of where he is strong. When a man's moralities clash with his self-interest, his so-called moralities lose every time. People who show interest in spiritual truths only when troubled are not interested at all. Foolish people have no difficulty explaining things they cannot understand."

91. When we associate with others we really associate with ourselves. We like or dislike in others whatever we like or dislike in ourselves. A man who is a danger to himself is attracted to other people who are also dangers to themselves and who are therefore a danger to the attracted man. Whoever builds his home next to an active volcano cannot complain of feeling threatened.

92. Asked a visitor to a class, "Why all this emphasis on self-study? What is wrong with every musician playing the music as he sees it?" The visitor was asked, "But what if he is unknowingly reading the music upside down?" Answered the visitor, "In that case he would recognize the discord." A student replied, "No, because he covers up the discord by calling it exciting music."

93. Wisdom is required when viewing someone who has brought suffering upon himself. View him as someone who is not yet capable of seeing how he himself pulled the house down upon his head. Then show him how to stop repeating his self-defeating behavior. Above all, do nothing which prevents the needed lesson from reaching his mind. Never approve of his self-pity or his attempts to blame others for his mistake. This is true compassion toward him.

94. The future is the unknown and the fearful to people. In a desperate attempt to feel secure by shaping the future according to personal desire, they only cause a wreck. The future does not unfold in obedience to personal demand, but by natural laws. By living within all natural laws one transcends time and is therefore both confident and indifferent toward the future. Imagine ocean waves which approach and break harmlessly around a skilled swimmer. That is how it is.

95. A farmer traded his wheat for some artificial gold, but not realizing his gullibility, he felt happy. One day when hungry he tried to trade it back for wheat, but no one would take it. But the strange part is that the farmer continued to trade wheat for artificial gold, never ever questioning anything.

96. Shake a compass as much as you like and its needle will always return to point in the right direction. Such is man's true nature, a nature cleansed of all that is nervous and unreliable. Onlookers may not realize that such a nature cannot really be shaken, but the owner of that nature knows and rests in the fact.

97. There was once a land inhabited by habitually ill people. One day an orchardist who lived in the distant hills sent the sufferers a message, saying, "I have a rare fruit which cures all ills. Make the journey up here and it is yours." But unfortunately it became a popular pastime for everyone to pretend he had obtained the curative fruit. What a tragic comedy. When two sick men met they loudly congratulated each other for being well!

98. A student wisely wrote down bits and pieces of collected information. Here are a few of them: "Every problem can be traced back to man's stubborn refusal to listen to anything but his stale memories. You can

insist upon having your own way, but you can also insist upon wearing gloves while playing the piano. There are many people who tell you more than they know. There is no indignation like the indignation of a sinner sinned against. When everything else fails, why not try the facts?"

99. A story was written about a man planning an expedition up the Amazon River. He was visited by overnight friends who promised to help with the plans the next morning. But when the man awakened at dawn his friends were gone. Lesson: Only one's own inner help is dependable in all circumstances. Build self-reliance.

100. To live rightly we must understand how Life actually works, which includes comprehension of cosmic laws. Start by realizing that Life does not respond to artificial needs and desires, for example, the desire for social power. Power-seeking is a vain attempt to prove false ideas about oneself, for instance, that one can control events. Life will have nothing to do with such self-defeating self-deception. Our real needs are as naturally abundant as colors in the countryside.

HOW THREE STUDENTS CLIMBED HIGHER

101. At the end of his talk to a study group a teacher asked, "What was the most helpful point you heard tonight?" Said one man, "The point that there is no better physician than a fact." Said a woman, "The idea that we must not accept excuses from ourselves." Said a third member, "The statement that our task is to get outside of ourselves."

102. One night Beethoven heard a series of knocks on his neighbor's door. His creative attitude toward the incident produced one of his famous concertos. It starts with four soft taps on a drum, which are then repeated throughout the composition. Likewise have a creative attitude toward whatever happens to you. Your plans do not work out? Know there is a Superior Plan for you. You do not know which way to turn? End the confusion by turning toward the Light. Right attitudes invite solutions.

103. An instructor was asked, "What is the difference between real and artificial stability?" Answer: "Real stability is not bothered by change, while false firmness quivers at the slightest deviation from the familiar. Don't call it stability if it shakes over a loss or over a sudden crisis, but call it an illusion of firmness. Authentic stability exists in your true nature. Who you are is quite enough for you, providing you really know who you are."

104. A mature and self-unified nature is the only solution to nervousness toward others. When we do not seek useless rewards from a social situation we do not tensely divide ourselves into what we are and what we want to appear to be. A pine tree in a grove of oak trees is not nervous about it, for its own nature is enough. These facts are the sure cure for social nervousness.

105. A teacher in an esoteric school used every opportunity to slip lessons to his pupils. One morning he was directing some students in placing rocks to form a border around the garden. One student asked the teacher to hand him some more rocks. Seeing the pupil's loaded arms the teacher said, "When you are ready to

carry more I will give you more." Everyone within hearing understood the lesson.

106. A doctor who had attended classes for many years stood up one evening to offer a few helpful comments. He concluded, "Why is it such a genuine pleasure to explore cosmic principles? Because they lead to clearness of understanding, and understanding is happiness itself."

107. A teacher instructed his pupils, "Between now and tomorrow I wish each of you to find a contradiction in yourself. For instance, you might find your face laughing over something that your emotions do not find funny. Remember, self-contradictions are both unconscious and wasteful. I once met a man who talked for a full hour to convince me he had conquered compulsive talking."

108. Self-instruction can be just as entertaining as a banquet or a holiday, providing the spirit is right. What is the right spirit? To not mind the loss of something you consider valuable. What is entertaining about that? What is entertaining about losing an artificial ruby in order to own a real one?

109. A frantic flying after the answer chases the answer away. The librarian of an esoteric school observed the study habits of one anxious student. Habitually, he checked out several books which he soon returned in exchange for new books. The tense student finally asked the librarian, "Can you tell me where I am going wrong?" The librarian told him, "Yes. You are too busy seeking help to receive it."

110. A jungle tribe in South America built a bridge made of rope across one of the rivers. On the far side

of the bridge was a trail leading to the city where the tribesmen traded their goods. Any boy or girl wishing to visit the city for the first time had to cross the bridge, which was shaky but perfectly safe. Our crossing of the cosmic bridge may shake us, but we finally see that we were perfectly safe all the time.

111. Regardless of how it may appear just now, everything you need to do for yourself can be done by yourself. Start by removing useless weights from your mind, just as a mountain climber ascends with as little equipment as possible. For example, drop the idea that any other human being has power to block your ascent.

112. Inquired a new student of the instructor, "What new value will we have as a result of our studies?" The teacher asked in return, "What new value does a haunted house have when all the ghosts are chased out?" You can chase out all the ghosts in your human relations.

113. Men drag everything down to their own low level of understanding. A resident of a dry prairie accidentally found himself on a mountain slope. There he saw a large and beautiful flower of many colors. Since he had known only the small and commonplace flowers of the prairie, the new flower appeared strange to him. Taking the flower, he carried it down to the prairie where he snipped off half the petals and threw dust over the remaining ones. "Now *there!*" he shouted with satisfaction. "There is a *real* flower!"

114. Obviously, man does things the hard way. He does everything the hard way because of failure to possess his one great possession—his real nature. He behaves foolishly and awkwardly simply because he has not learned how to act naturally. The owner of a

house has no need to enter it by climbing clumsily through a window. Whatever is natural is also easy.

115. An absent member of a study group wrote to the class, "I gave myself a definite assignment. I was to think about the value of disillusionment. A small child may be disappointed in realizing that an exciting stage play is not real, but it is a healthy arousal. We must realize how numerous our illusions are, then have the mental maturity to see through them. For example, we must not be gullible when seeking help. The only man who can help another get out of trouble is a man who is not in trouble with himself." Be impressed by this last sentence.

116. When thinking about religion or politics or anything else you might say, "I believe this is true." Pause a moment right here to do some healthy self-investigating. Ask, "Would I feel guilty or insecure by not taking this as true?" Or you might ask, "Would I miss a feeling of excitement by dropping this belief?" This intelligent probing helps you to see things as *they* are, not as *you* are. It is like removing an obsolete pair of distorting glasses to see things clearly with your own eyes.

117. Imagine yourself standing outside on bare ground. See what is supporting you? The entire world. This you can see with your eyes. But you are also supported by an invisible world far greater than the earth. You may not see it as yet but it is there. Open your inner eyes. See it. *This invisible world can be seen.*

118. An earnest climber should remain aware of how dark forces try to tug him away from the upward trail. His very recognition of their harmful influence is enough

to cancel it, just as an observing policeman scatters criminals. One student felt tempted by discouragement. He banished it by remembering that he had nothing to return to but his old and meaningless ways. Let your own awareness keep you on the upward trail.

119. Because a man's physical eyes are open he assumes his inner eyes are also wide open, that is, he attributes cosmic consciousness to himself. He believes he is promoting principles when he is really defending delusions. Becoming aware of this deficiency in himself, a member of a study group went into action. He profited by examining just why human beings foolishly love darkness more than light.

120. Why are human beings lost? Imagine yourself as part of a group of tourists being guided through one of the huge underground caverns in the United States. As the tourists proceed along the path the guide instructs them to turn either left or right. But one argumentative tourist insists upon turning in the direction he prefers. He is no different from millions of people who fearfully insist that they know more than the Guiding Truth. Now do you know why human beings are lost?

AIM FOR THE
WORTHWHILE TARGET

121. An archer wanting to hit a target does not aim for the ground. Man aims for the ground when thinking that social schemes or lofty words can uplift human happiness. To hit the target there must be individual self-study accompanied by a willingness to change whatever must be changed. All else is futile— as men in futility dimly realize. Now you can start hitting the target.

122. Confessed an inquirer, "All my life I have been told that I must believe and have faith, but I have never known what that means." She was told, "For a change, stop trying to believe something. Can you stop believing that happiness depends upon a certain event happening to you?"

123. Ordinary systems advise people to not be afraid. As elementary advice it is all right, but higher counsel exists. It tells a scared person, "Go ahead and be just as scared as you really are, for presently you have no choice. But add intelligent action to your fear by seeking to understand and dissolve it. Be like the brave knight in armor who discovered that the dragon was afraid of *him.*"

124. Imagine a historian reading the first paragraph of a rare book he has just obtained. His eagerness mounts with the realization that here at last is the confirming information he has sought for years. This eagerness also comes to those who read truthful books. What is right in the book corresponds with what is right in the reader, dynamically uplifting his level of cosmic understanding. A new world is just ahead of the reader.

125. An advanced student contributed this in class: "When someone's words or manners suggest he wants to give you something, try to discover what he wants to get from you. Inside that gift package may be a trap. If you meet someone who snaps that this is an unkind way to look at people, look at that someone with special sharpness."

126. What endangers a man is his own psychological level. A person walking at night near the edge of a cliff endangers himself, even though he believes he

is safe. Only consciousness of his actual psychological level can rescue anyone from peril.

127. Four students were told just where they were standing in their own way. The first heard, "You take advice as personal criticism, instead of as helpful information." The next man received, "Correct the wandering of your attention while here in class." The third student was told, "You must prefer true answers to exciting ones." The last pupil heard, "Realize that a glum spirit is as out of place here as a goat in an art gallery."

128. Mental pain can be turned into insight. That insight then ends the pain. At the first appearance of pain you must stand aside to simply watch it flow through you. The very watching is a type of detachment which weakens the pain's mechanical flow. You understand a raging flood by observing it from the riverbank, not by letting it carry you away. Experiment with this.

129. A speaker ended his talk by saying, "I will give you two ideas to think about until we meet again. We mistakenly see things not as they are, but as we are. A little self-arousal induces more self-arousal, so arouse yourself right now."

130. People do not have what they could have because they do not ask for it. They do not ask for it because they do not know enough to ask. They do not know enough to ask because they insist they already have what they want. But here is the strangest part. A man drops through the trapdoor a dozen times a day but never asks, "Why do I always return to this same spot?"

131. Free yourself. That frees you of others. Are you now unfree of others? Do you go places you don't want to go and spend money you don't want to spend because others expect it of you? Why do you live under the pain and resentment of living up to the expectations of others? You need not. You need not feel like a sparrow in a cage of hawks. The door is not locked. Push it outward. Free yourself.

132. A young prince of Persia had to find a document to prove his right to the throne. He finally found it hidden inside a plain and ordinary cap he habitually wore while riding his horse. What you may think has been lost has not been lost. It is simply out of sight at the present moment. Search! See!

133. A student read to a new class a letter from their traveling teacher. The letter read in part, "Your present ways of thinking have not solved your problems and they never will. They won't because they can't. You suspect this, but must go much deeper—so deep your mind and spirit have a tremendous urge to think in a totally new way. This noble way is known by others, and can be known by you."

134. Don't let other people tell you what you want. You don't at all want what society says you want. You don't want social popularity; you want to live contentedly with yourself. You don't want to conquer the world; you want calm self-command. You don't want a sense of superiority; you want to know what life is all about. Be like the hungry man who refused a ticket to the theater because he needed food, not entertainment.

135. When Thomas More's book *Utopia* was first published a large number of readers believed that

Utopia was an actual country. Some even planned to send missionaries there to convert the natives. Because a man fails to check the facts he wastes his time in illusory aims. One of them is the wish to save others from delusion before he has rescued himself. Know that facts prevent follies.

136. Self-limited men reject anyone who urges them to go beyond themselves. In one country the only known vegetable was squash. The citizens tried to vary things with squash soup, squash salad, squash pie, but it was still a dull menu. One day a visiting botanist tried to tell them about potatoes and beets and carrots, but the very unfamiliarity of the words scared the people. As the botanist left town, the wise men of the village agreed, "Most men are honest, but every once in awhile you meet a charlatan like him."

137. How strange that people expect to feel right without thinking right. They believe they can think any way they choose and then have pleasant emotions. That is like believing there is no relationship between a father and his son. Whoever wishes to feel good should ponder the connection between thoughts and emotions. You will then feel good when in the company of other people.

138. On the school grounds a teacher was leading the children in physical exercises. For the third exercise the pupils were told to jump up and down. One boy added extra movements, such as flinging his arms about and shaking his head. When asked about it he replied, "That is what jumping is to *me.*" Out of such an attitude does true individuality arise. What is true individuality? It is to live from one's original nature in a way that harms neither the individual nor others.

139. Much can be learned about a person's level of cosmic maturity by noticing his reaction after hearing a truth-lecture. Anyone who challenges the speaker is vainly trying to prove himself as intelligent as the speaker. One who gushes, "Simply marvelous!" will not be back, for he or she loves dramatic expression more than healing fact. Those who criticize the presented truths are trying to reduce their fear of them. But whoever quietly ponders the message, even though unclear in himself, is using the occasion wisely.

140. A person who has attained cosmic intelligence resembles a woman wisely shopping in a supermarket. Out of the thousands of items, she knows which ones she wants and which ones are valueless to her. Most human beings are unwise shoppers who rush down the aisles, throwing almost anything into their baskets. They then complain of having so many unwanted and expensive things in their lives! We can learn to value only the valuable.

HOW TO FIND AN
AUTHENTIC TEACHER

141. Qualifications for teaching cosmic truth are vastly different from qualifications in ordinary life. In ordinary life a person can teach science or history because other people declare he is legally qualified. But cosmic qualification comes only through personal discovery, not through the approval of others. It is obvious enough. The only man who can show others how to conquer inner dragons is one who has himself conquered the dragons.

142. A study group of ten people met regularly in the home of one of the members. They discussed the

great truths which set men free, moreover, they were actually freeing themselves. Next door there lived some people who complained, "Why is life so hard?" and "Why is there no solution?" One day one of the complainers stepped outside where he met a member of the study group. The complainer remarked, "I understand you have a class for finding life's answers. A noble aim! Well, good-bye, we have just bought a new boat we are eager to sail."

143. Ordinary thought cannot cure human wrongness any more than a medical book can produce health. Knowing the words is not the same as experiencing the healing. Sermons and laws and reforms cannot uplift human nature because they originate on the level of contrived thought which can never rise above itself. Wondrously, the very seeing of the impotence of ordinary thought awakens a new nature which is truly innocent of wrongdoing.

144. A lazy and careless man never kept his watch at the right time. He felt a twisted pleasure at giving people the wrong time, especially the large number of people he classified as enemies. But strangely, he also planned his own schedule by the incorrect watch. And whenever he missed something by being late he angrily blamed the first person he saw. So here you have a good example of someone who cannot see that whatever he does to others he also does to himself.

145. A person who says he is bored with the world would be shocked to learn the full significance of his statement. There is no individual *and* his world; the individual *is* his world. So just as it is the nature of a desert to be dry, it is the nature of the bored person to be boring. However, I would not tell him this unless you can run fast.

146. Said a teacher, "I will tell you something you do not know. Relatives and friends and strangers are completely different kinds of human beings than you think they are. They are so different you would feel shocked as if by lightning to see them as they really are. You mistake what *they* are because you mistake what *you* are. You are foolishly and dangerously deceived because you fear to face the disturbing facts about human nature. You think people are polite, never realizing that a dog in the kitchen is always polite."

147. Imagine a stranger in town who asks several residents for directions for reaching the library. Each resident believes he supplies accurate directions, but in fact each of them sends the stranger the wrong way. This is precisely what happens when we ask our conditioned minds for directions. And this is why we must contact Cosmic Mind which always supplies accurate directions.

148. You may have seen photographs of wild animals which were taken at night with special cameras. The animals tripped a wire which recorded their activities at den or stream. The photographers did not know what interesting scenes they had until the pictures were developed. Likewise, though it may seem that you are working in the dark with these studies you are still making definite progress. Your patience and persistence will develop into valuable self-knowledge.

149. Wherever you may be, only one factor determines whether you are in a light or a dark place. That factor is the light or dark state of your own mind. A lighted lamp set out in the night is not penetrated by surrounding darkness.

150. A traveling teacher wrote a letter to his students. Part of it read, "Think of fifteen minutes spent in reading

a book of cosmic knowledge. Think of another fifteen minutes spent in discussion with each other. That thirty minutes can help you to stop repeating all the mistakes you have made in the past. Is it a profitable thirty minutes?"

151. An experiment in a lecture hall proved the shallowness of human minds. Two speakers on the subject of ecology were presented the same night to an audience. One speaker was tall, handsome, with an impressive personality. The other speaker was plain in appearance and quiet in speech. A poll showed that most of the listeners believed that the dynamic speaker was the more competent of the two. He was in fact a professional actor whose speech contained many errors which his bluffing manner cleverly concealed. The plain speaker was the ecology expert.

152. Commented a member of a study group, "The tragedy is that men and women inhabit a world of conflict and confusion." Responded the instructor, "The greater tragedy is that men and women know no other world than the confused one they insist upon inhabiting." Resolve that you will find the existing higher world.

153. Some cunning spies lured a scientist to a secret laboratory located in a secluded area. Treated like a guest, the scientist failed to realize that he was in fact a prisoner, so he gave valuable information to the spies. But finally seeing through the hoax, he quietly escaped one night. Psychologically, a man who is captured by delusions does not know he is. That is why he is. He must see through the hoax of attractive delusions, for they are traitors. When exposing the hoax, he takes command of his life.

154. Some people feel they have nothing worthwhile to give to Truth in exchange for the royal estate which Truth will give them. Nothing is more easily solved. Truth asks for neither gifts nor compliments. Truth asks for your willingness to understand—nothing more. Even a bit of willingness will serve at first. Willingness grows in size, just as a river increases its width as it flows forward by receiving smaller streams.

155. Insight into the need for self-rescue arouses great energy for that self-rescue. One man became aware of his fear of disappointing other people. He quivered at the thought of their disapproving frowns and critical words. Though at first shocked at seeing his weakness, he turned the shock into energy for becoming a truly independent man who feared no one.

156. A man who resolves, "I will not lose my temper tomorrow" will lose his temper tomorrow. He is frustrated by a lack of self-knowledge. One liberated man explained before a class, "A mere resolve is on the level of thought, and a thought is only part of a man. One wheel of a car cannot repair another wheel. The very understanding of this lifts us to the higher level of corrective consciousness."

157. The ability to foresee consequences and thereby avoid unpleasant ones is a characteristic of a cosmically mature mind. Such a mind resembles a motorist whose sharp eyesight reveals every turn in the road ahead, giving him quiet skill and confidence. An immature mind insists it knows the road when it does not, causing skids. But you can learn to avoid unpleasant human involvements.

158. A class in Indiana heard, "You must see your secret desperation so clearly that it is not a secret to you any more. This replaces self-deception with a bright ray of self-honesty. Then, of equal importance, you must see that your very desperation is a barrier to self-awakening. Desperation indicates a fondness for the very ideas which cause desperation. You cling to your own harm, like a child who refuses to give up a dangerous toy. Detect and give up dangerous toys. Think about all this."

159. A woman was seeking semiprecious stones in the desert, but having little success. While walking along a low ridge she suddenly lost her footing and slid into a ravine—where she found an open treasure of stones. Every loss of psychological footing, perhaps an embarrassment or a bewilderment, places us in a position to find what we really want—our real nature.

160. An ancient legend told about a village with an interesting name. When translated, the name came out as *The Village Of Those Who Use Dissatisfaction Rightly.* Its citizens had the happy habit of correcting troublesome conditions instead of grumbling over them. Anyone can use dissatisfaction rightly by seeing that the cause is within, not outside.

LOOK FOR LOFTY BENEFITS

161. A visitor to a country noticed something curious. Each day a new flag was set atop the king's castle. The visitor was finally informed by a citizen, "We have a good and wise king. Each flag is the day's message which can be read by all who see and understand. One flag informs us of the right time to harvest our fields, while another invites us to a royal banquet." It is quite

possible for us to see and understand the equally good and wise cosmic messages. One result is freedom from unkind people.

162. Imagine a child trying to study the stars with a toy telescope. Unable to see fascinating details of the stars, he soon loses interest in the upward gaze. Now imagine a man trying to study cosmic facts with his immature mind. Seeing everything through personal desires and habits, he concludes that nothing of interest exists except his own familiar world. Tragically, he judges everything by himself. What fascinating facts could you, the reader, give him?

163. An unhappy princess went to a wise man for advice. After questioning her for awhile, the wise man wrote a single sentence on a slip of paper which he gave to the princess. "Read and ponder this every day," advised the wise man. Doing so, the princess felt a new lightness. The sentence read, "Never accept the examples of living thrust upon you by other people."

164. Imagine yourself standing on a hill where you see a small fire break out in the distant valley below. You see it but know you cannot stop it. However, you might find some way to arouse the residents of the valley who could then quench the fire. That is the position of a man who sees things as they are. He tries to arouse people into action toward their perilous fires of ignorance and insolence.

165. A student contributed to the class, "I will tell you where I made a major mistake. I believed I had already attained that which it is possible for me to attain. I was a foolish child dreaming I was an intelligent adult. How intelligent was it for me to live in secret fear of everything?"

166. A man appears intelligent to himself because he has only one viewpoint of himself—his own. But from the cosmic viewpoint he appears quite different, so different he would be astonished at his vanity in calling himself intelligent. After explaining these ideas to a class, a teacher added, "An awakened man does not see you as you see yourself—for which you can be very grateful. That is why he can help you attain real intelligence."

167. An advertisement pictured a dozen keys and a lock. Beneath them the question was asked, "Which key fits the lock?" Anyone studying the keys learned the answer, for some keys were obviously too large or too short. Careful mind-study reveals the right mental key for daily living. The right thought creates no conflict, feels comfortable, fits naturally into whatever we encounter. Healthy thoughts create healthy human events.

168. A young man was hired as an apprentice in a sign-painting shop. The foreman noticed that the youth habitually made his signs so fancy and so decorative that the actual message could not be read easily. Taking the young man aside the foreman counseled gently, "Above all else, make everything clear." Above all else, we wish to make our minds and lives clear.

169. Inner slaveries are unseen, which is why they are so painful, like stumbling over a chain in the dark. One of the worst slaveries is an attempt to please someone in order to keep him or her within your circle of security. Please yourself. It is not wrong to please yourself in the cosmic way for that is the same as having the contentment of self-knowledge. In this state there is no insecurity which tries to hold anyone.

170. A lecture on the subject of understanding went, "When confusion and frustration reach the breaking point, a marvelous opportunity awaits—if you do not fight, but seek to understand. If you do not know who you are, your life can begin to change—if you do not fight, but seek to understand." As a result of hearing this, many people gave up fighting in exchange for understanding. Everything turned sunny, including their human relations.

171. A widely-acclaimed scholar was asked a question. He replied without hesitation, "Considering the uninhibited complexities of the prevailing proposition, with its peripheral ramifications, it seems inevitable to require comprehension to reside in a systematic scrutiny of human aberration as it correlates to the consequences of psychological permissiveness." He said this because he did not know how to say, "I don't know the answer."

172. Human beings do not understand even the simplest of facts about their unhappy condition. They fail to see the link between their preference for fantasy and their nervousness. The power of fantasy is so strong that people think they are having a good time when they are merely wasting money. It is like the woman at a party who timidly asked a waiter, "Am I enjoying myself?"

173. A teacher told a class of new pupils who would live at the school, "For the rest of the day I want you to be perfectly sincere with each other." The pupils nodded and left. Shaking his head, the teacher sighed to an advanced student, "See? They always fail the test. Like everyone else they not only assume they know what it means to be sincere but believe they can practice it." The student replied, "By this time they have already

deceived each other in sly attempts to get the best rooms for themselves."

174. No man who really understands human nature as it is can ever be injured by human nature as it is. So we are really wounded by a lack of both self-knowledge and other-knowledge. A belief that we already have insight into people cannot save us; only actual insight can do that. A stunned soldier on the battlefield may dream he is safe at home, but the bullets do not believe in his dream. Insight into people is a reliable servant of yours.

175. The invisible roots of a tree stretch down toward water in order to make the visible tree healthy and natural. As an aid to your progress, remember this illustration of how the invisible contributes to the visible.

176. A member of a study group in Kansas reported, "Several weeks ago I misplaced a flashlight. A search of the house failed to locate it. Two days later I remembered I had used it in a corner of the backyard, where it was finally located. Our lives are like that. We have forgotten where we have placed our source of light, but with diligence we can make the recovery."

177. There was once a lark who liked to associate with a hawk. The smaller bird greatly admired the hawk's savage power. But one day the hawk gazed in a peculiar way at the lark, causing the smaller bird to fly away in fear. "You were fortunate this time," an owl later told the lark, "so don't go back." The lark wondered aloud, "But why was I attracted to such a fierce creature?" The owl explained, "Because you have more of a hawk's nature in yourself than you realize." Study this deep idea.

178. The sensing of Truth is always faint at first, like approaching a flower garden and catching our first scent. This sensing comes of itself as a result of remaining on the road in spite of all discouragements and bewilderments.

179. It is difficult to erase writing on a rock, but easy to erase whatever is written on a blackboard. Happily, the human mind resembles a blackboard. Incorrect information acquired in the past can be erased instantly to make room for the reliable. Here is a reliable fact: You can be resourceful in finding yourself because you really do have resources to uncover.

180. A young schoolgirl asked permission to water some flowers displayed on a desk. The teacher thanked the girl but said it would be both useless and unnecessary. Explained the teacher, "The flowers are plastic." Unaware human beings waste themselves in activities which can never yield real cosmic blossoms.

THE WOLVES AND THE SHEEP

181. Two wolves were discussing a flock of sheep. "To show you how stupid they are," chuckled one wolf, "they think I am their friend. They actually *pay me* for phony advice on how to avoid wolves." Laughed the other wolf, "That's nothing. I actually make them *feel guilty* over avoiding wolves!"

182. You can contribute everything you need to yourself. This is because you are a miniature representative of the Cosmic Whole, and this representative contains within itself all the elements of the Cosmic Whole. It is similar to a sycamore tree in the United States which has every characteristic of every other sycamore tree in

the world. Your contribution to yourself is of a special kind. It consists of *recognition* of what you already have. And what you have is unlimited inner power.

183. Quite often just the right word at the right time is enough to explode error. One teacher gave his class a short talk on the topic of unnecessary thoughts. He showed how useless thoughts, such as annoyance and self-condemnation, waste valuable mental energy. This struck one attentive listener with great force. The listener commented later, "When it comes to annoyance or self-condemnation, I have much better things to do with my mind."

184. An instructor told some new students, "Do not expect these teachings to match what you already take as true. That is like demanding that the road turn left instead of right, or run up instead of down. Follow the road wherever it leads. It knows where it is going."

185. A scientific expedition established a camp alongside the Orinoco River in the tropical forests of Venezuela. Faulty communications cut them off from their source of supply in a distant village. A native runner managed to reach the village, which restored supplies. If even one part of us can make contact with our source of psychic supply, that is enough to attract everything needed. This includes wisdom for handling people rightly.

186. Remember that wrongness always wears a disguise, like a saboteur in a policeman's uniform. Wrongness, evil, treachery, cunningly present themselves as something right or necessary or justifiable. In other words, wrongness never tells the truth. When doubtful about society's ways, let this fact roam through your mind, and it will protect you against deceitful people.

187. To make sure that his writings were easy to understand, British author Jonathan Swift read his manuscripts aloud to simple and uneducated people. He did not want to be profound; he wanted to be clear. Likewise, a man need not try to be profound or impressive to himself; he needs only to be understood by himself.

188. If only you will realize how little you have in common with society's disorder. If only you will realize that you can be in the world and yet not participate in its weary ways. This realization comes with the restoration of one's natural citizenship. A citizen of a peaceful nation is undisturbed by the wars of other countries.

189. A fugitive from a mad society finally made it to the Celestial City. When asked about his success he told about his Journey through the Valley of Humiliation. "I was first humiliated by having to toss out everything I had called my wisdom and intelligence. The second humiliation was to no longer believe I was as likeable as I liked to believe. The third humiliation was to see how little control I really had over myself. There were others, and without them I would not have made it here."

190. Because the unknown has a certain attraction, people eagerly explore strange jungles and mountains. But they are not so eager toward inner exploration, for it seems to threaten what they call their psychological security. One inner explorer helped himself by realizing that his self-protective attitudes protected nothing, to the contrary, they kept him tense. So remember, the secret of success is to let yourself go, not knowing where you will go. One day you will always go right.

191. Cosmic nature and your nature are just right for each other, in fact they are the two covers of the same book. But we have acquired an artificial nature that causes conflict by claiming independence and superiority for itself. Use these facts as handy erasers to get rid of that uncomfortable claim.

192. "To help you," a spiritual teacher told three seekers, "I must tell each of you something you do not want to hear." The men agreed to this, so the teacher continued, "One of you is a hypocrite, another is arrogant, and the third man will be told of his fault tomorrow." The three men stood up to say in unison, "See you tomorrow." Those who persist in self-discovery will find freedom.

193. When you meet another person he instantly searches your face and manner to see what kind of person you are. If your face is a silent invitation to plunder, he will subtly try to get all he can. What kind of silent message do you transmit? Self-information provides a relaxation which is not weakness and an alertness which is not tension. Your high psychic level is total protection, for we can be nipped by wolves only when running with the pack.

194. English chemist Humphry Davy invented the safety lamp, which he declined to patent. Instead, he gave its benefits freely to the world. The light of Truth is equally generous. It gives itself freely to all who ask. Just ask. Do it now. You will receive.

195. A soldier on night patrol became separated from the rest of his squad, A few minutes later he saw a line of soldiers following a trail through the woods, so he fell in at the end of the line. He was horrified to hear one of the soldiers speak the language of the enemy.

He quietly fell out of line. Because of mental darkness we ally ourselves with enemies, including sour attitudes and refusals to learn. You are now changing all this.

196. A husband and wife, both troubled by life, traveled a long distance to consult a wise man. The wise man's disciples told the couple that any counsel they received would be a thousand times more profound than it appeared to be. The husband asked the wise man, "What must we do to rescue ourselves?" The answer came, "You must love Truth enough to let it change you into what *it* is."

197. Here is the formula for inner success: Right teacher plus right student. A right teacher is one who really knows what he is talking about. A right student is one whose preliminary work enables him to recognize a right teacher as right. When they meet a healthy atmosphere develops, just as a match and a candle meet to create light.

198. What we take as disturbance can be used for enlightenment. A tired traveler fell asleep in a strange land. When a flash of lightning disturbed his sleep he was at first tempted to feel anger toward the lightning. But then, with its light, he saw he had been sleeping near a cave of dangerous animals. That made him grateful to the disturbing lightning.

199. The more unusual an experience the more value it has for those who are tired of self-shackles. The entire secret is to take the unusual or the unpleasant experience with conscious attention, not with habitual fear or resentment. Self-shackles are cut with something stronger than shackles, and conscious attention is a thousand times stronger. Practice this secret power.

200. A demon wrote to a demon friend, "Do you know what keeps us in business? It is the lunatic habit of human beings to take another's word for something instead of investigating for themselves. In my long career of drawing people into the net I have never met a truly independent thinker. They exist all right, but thank heaven they are rare. People are like a line of soldiers standing in tense uncertainty because the captain is absent. So get your human allies to appear authoritative, and human gullibility will do the rest."

THE SAFETY OF A WHOLE MIND

201. Have you ever watched a person's face struggle with itself because he is caught between two opposing thoughts? This is a good example of mental division, a topic requiring careful study. Start your study by realizing that living in mental division is like living in a cage with two rival lions. Out of this realization arises the urge to escape the cage to live with a single and whole mind, which provides safety in all situations.

202. A famous lecturer stood up to speak to an audience of several thousand people. He urged everyone to rely upon heavenly power, to live with personal courage and confidence. He told a story about his own successful search for peace and security. Afterward, while walking to the parking lot, he sighed to someone, "Thank heaven I have the support of so many loyal friends."

203. A man can say he knows, but does his private life prove it? An archer is judged by the accuracy of his arrows, not by the fancy bow he displays. What an ordinary man thinks he knows, an awakened man really knows, including the facts about human nature.

204. An airplane was circling over a section of the Caribbean Sea when the pilot looked down to notice something strange. He saw the underwater ruins of ancient buildings. This led to a series of exciting discoveries in underseas archeology. The ruins had been there for centuries, but could be seen only by someone high above them. As we stand above our usual selves we sight new possibilities and make exciting discoveries, such as confidence in public.

205. "Today I will give you five guides to happiness," a teacher told his class. "Aim your whole mind toward psychic unfoldment. Observe your actual motives for doing anything. Daily clear your mind of useless thoughts. Place the invisible world before the visible. Become fascinated with self-discovery."

206. Our attention is habitually on objects of desire. Why not place it on objects of need? Someone may desire applause, but he needs the keys to the kingdom. We need right placement of attention, and we need an attention as intense as when opening a gift.

207. A class member going on vacation was given an assignment by the teacher. The student was to return with a short but meaningful message for increasing the light. The student returned to state to the class, "Any unpleasant fact about yourself you can bear to face can be eliminated as a fact about yourself. Any unpleasant fact about yourself you cannot bear to face will continue to be a fact about yourself." The class nodded in understanding and appreciation.

208. Imagine a diner entering a cafe. Accidentally, he picks up yesterday's menu. He eagerly anticipates the foods listed. He is then disappointed when the waitress explains his error. Man frustrates himself by

61

desiring a repetition of yesterday's thrills. He really needs only whatever each new day serves, for his own nature is equally new each day—if only he would see it.

209. A thought is painful only when allowed to persist in the mind. With knowledge of the mind you can learn to drop painful thoughts. This is not the same as suppressing uncomfortable thoughts, which is what most people do. A thought can be dropped only after seeing it clearly, as when awareness of a hot kettle makes you drop it. Painful thoughts about people can end.

210. A member of a study group raised her hand to say to the teacher, "A comment of yours earlier in the evening caught me by surprise. You said we must have courage enough to give up the superficial pleasure of grief. That means that grief supplies a strange and damaging kind of comfort." Responded the teacher, "Yes. The objective is to pass through the tunnel of grief, not to build a house in it."

211. A polar bear would suffer in an African jungle because his environment is not in harmony with his nature. We suffer from the jungle of society because it is unnatural to what we really are. But we can change our psychological environment by changing ourselves. When doing this we are astonished to discover that our environment and our nature were the same things, so in fact we formerly suffered only from ourselves. What a liberating lesson!

212. Someone stated, "Sometimes a book offers an especially deep paragraph. How can we read it with maximum understanding?" Answer: "Give full attention to one sentence at a time. Isolate it for a moment, reading slowly and thoughtfully. Do the same with the next sentence. But at the same time try to see

connections between sentences so that the main idea of the paragraph becomes clear."

213. Suppose you saw your neighbor frantically mopping up a flood of water on the kitchen floor, while leaving the faucet wide open. You would think it ridiculous. Man's psychic ways are equally absurd. He races around trying to clean up the effects of his folly, but ignores the causes. A wise man turns off the faucet of mechanical living in favor of conscious action.

214. Asked a new student, "How can we abolish the habitual self which causes so many painful problems?" Answered the teacher, "Coming to the end of habitual thought is the same as coming to the end of the habitual self, for the self is built out of repetitious thought. The end of the thought-self is also the end of all problems and pains and perplexities. So how do we end habitual thought? By learning what it means to have a conscious mind."

215. A woman was fond of feeding the birds that visited her yard. She observed that different foods attracted different kinds of birds. One week she wished to attract more bluebirds, succeeding by setting out the foods they liked in particular. A wise individual reflects, "The attitudes I set out attract certain kinds of people into my day. True and right attitudes will attract only those with a fondness for truth. To attract more quality in social relations, I must set out higher attitudes."

216. If you wish to know your future, study yourself. Knowledge about the original seed provides wisdom about the nature of the forthcoming fruit. A man's future develops out of his own nature. To change your future, change yourself.

217. Some prisoners of war were confined to rooms on the lower level of a castle. Every morning the captors were dismayed to find that at least one prisoner had escaped during the night. The prisoners had a happy secret. They had discovered a secret underground passage leading from the castle to the distant woods. Spiritually, there is a way out of a confining life. You may not have found it as yet, but it is there, ready for your discovery and use. You will then escape from troublesome people.

218. A couple attended a truth-talk. On the way home the woman complained, "He was not too original. I can't remember it but he repeated one sentence several times." The man agreed, "I don't recall it either but I know it prevented him from giving a sparkling talk." The sentence neither could remember was, "You shall know the truth and the truth shall make you free."

219. Society's measurement of intelligence is as false as society itself. Real intelligence can be measured by the number of things from which a man need not escape. A man spends half his time trying to get out of what he fell into through greed and ignorance. A fish swims into a net because it cannot understand the consequences of a net. A man struggles to escape the consequences of being what he is, rarely wondering whether he might change his nature. Change your nature and you will change all else.

220. A magnificent building called the Temple of Light stood a short distance from a road traveled by thousands of men and women every day. A sign on the temple invited everyone to enter and rest. But the burdened travelers were so distracted by their various destinations that few accepted the invitation.

BENEFICIAL FACTS ABOUT
A STUDY GROUP

221. A student on vacation wrote to another member of the class, "Do you know what attracted me to the group from the very start? It was the complete absence of compromise with Truth. In the past I attended weak groups which simply tried to please everyone. I saw what was happening. Under the disguise of helping people, the groups were actually encouraging self-destructive egotism. So I appreciate the bluntly honest atmosphere in which we meet. I am sure that you sense, as do I, that this is authentic compassion."

222. A new fact which a person cannot understand or does not wish to understand will be either distorted or scorned. This is because the familiar and mechanical parts of his mind are in command instead of his conscious parts. He is like someone who gets into trouble by listening to the advice of a treacherous stranger instead of to a wise friend. Your wise friend is Truth.

223. In an excited moment a foolish man bought a tiger. So for a long time he wore himself out trying to protect himself from the tiger. Higher teachings show you how to stop buying tigers.

224. A familiar theme for a mystery story is one in which someone must stay overnight in a haunted house in order to inherit a fortune. He bravely endures the horrible ghosts and weird shrieks. In the light of dawn he sees that it was all a hoax played upon him by greedy conspirators. In the spiritual life, the human house seems haunted only as long as understanding is absent. Let consciousness dawn. The ghosts will vanish.

225. A somewhat timid woman finally found strength to raise her hand and ask her first question in class: "What part does beauty play in this higher world?" She and the class heard, "Beauty is a state in which you are totally free of the need to make an impression upon others or upon yourself."

226. The problem is, a man's wild imagination can soar higher than his level of being. Able to think about goodness he deceives himself by believing that he lives what he thinks. This self-deception enables him to sing like a nightingale while pouncing like a hawk. To end the pouncing he must cease to think of himself as either a nightingale or a hawk, which gives him a chance to be a normal human being. Review this profound idea.

227. One sign of cosmic dawning is to realize that we are doing things we really do not want to do. It is like a woman attending a party, with all the usual artificial friendliness, who suddenly realizes she would rather be home doing things which really interest her. Encourage your own cosmic dawning. What are you doing that you wish you did not have to do? Come home.

228. A light and unburdened spirit wins over the walls of misunderstanding, just as a balloon rises above a brick wall. So pursue your esoteric education seriously and yet cheerfully, patiently and yet eagerly. This attracts true power and pleasure.

229. A multitude of people came to the gate of a palace, seeking to see the king. The gate-keeper listened patiently as some displayed their lists of demands upon the king, while others claimed eligibility for entrance because of their personal goodness. Some wealthy people

tried to bribe the gate-keeper, while one group tried to influence him by wearing impressive uniforms. But only those without arguments and self-serving motives were allowed to see the king.

230. The topic of cosmic secrets came up in a group discussion. The teacher remarked, "They are secrets only because we have not directed our energies toward their discovery. Here is one such secret for your discovery. Noninterference with the natural flow of life is a great secret for cosmic success."

231. A traveler in Norway who spoke only French asked a shopkeeper for directions to a nearby town. The shopkeeper asked a customer to translate the Frenchman's request into Norwegian. The translation was so faulty it sent the traveler in the wrong direction. Cosmic language tries to direct us to a higher destination, but our minds translate wrongly. Correction should begin today. Start by wanting a higher life.

232. Said a member of a study group, "By accident I once found myself in a peculiar place. It was a meeting attended by very dignified people who were promoting the most nonsensical beliefs imaginable. It was incredible. You know what I discovered? People have the most enthusiasm for ideas they don't understand." Agreed another member, "Yes. The very vagueness enables them to add their own self-pleasing myths to the established confusion. A ship in a fog makes the most noise." Remember all this.

233. Resentment boils up in people far more often than they want to admit. Self-harming resentment decreases as insight increases. A man resentfully feels that other people are always telling him what to do. This condition exists because he has never learned to tell

himself what to do, that is, he has not learned to live from his free nature. Only a caged bird complains of domination by other caged birds.

234. A teacher told his pupils, "A man who really knows the answers has no need for confirmation from others. Give up the false pleasure of having others agree with your pet beliefs."

235. People complain that they don't know what to do about their troubled lives. That is like a man at a mountain brook complaining of thirst. We know very well what we must do. We must acquire the life-saving facts and act on them. For instance, we must see that self-study precedes self-change.

236. There was once a parrot who had the same habit as many human beings. He did not live by the laws of his own nature, but carelessly imitated whatever he saw. One day the parrot observed some travelers at a border station being treated roughly by the guards. Also wishing to cross the border, the parrot sighed and started to fly down to the station. "Foolish bird!" shouted a passing owl who interrupted the parrot's flight. "Wake up! You are not under oppressive laws. Live by the laws of the sky. Fly over!" Your true nature is free from oppressive human conditions.

237. Like excited dogs tugging at their leashes, men strain toward their own disasters. It continues to happen because men rarely see that the attainment of an exciting desire simply makes them the slave of the next exciting desire. You are setting yourself free.

238. A person who does not see his actual condition will dwell in a corresponding degree of illusion about his condition. The deeper he has wandered into the jungle the more he will assume that tigers are sheep and that

weeds are roses. He has one great opportunity. He can see the jungle as a jungle, which will arouse new energy and higher intelligence for getting out.

239. Explained a teacher, "Tension is one result of self-contradiction. For example, a man is tense when pretending to understand something he does not really understand." Commented a student, "It is strange how people do not see the connection between pretense and tension. It is even stranger that they think pretense is necessary. Above pretense dwells true power and pleasure."

240. Carried away by custom, man rarely wonders whether there might be more to life than that disclosed by eyes and ears. This is why one teacher often started and ended his lectures with the declaration, "Examine your life!"

THE VALUE OF LIVING CONSCIOUSLY

241. While camping in the forest with his parents, a boy wandered away and became lost. When found several hours later he was asked why he failed to obtain permission to explore around. He answered, "I was afraid you would say no because I might get lost." Men and women sense the wrongness of some kinds of behavior, but still do it. With conscious living we never wander into hazardous conditions, such as harmful human involvements.

242. Imagine someone trying to open a lock with the wrong key. Instead of admitting he has the wrong key he insists indignantly that the *lock* is wrong. Do you know people who lock themselves out of a good life by justifying themselves like this?

243. A seeker visited a wise man to complain, "I have endured incredible hardships in search of true wisdom. But in spite of travels through Egypt and Syria, India and Tibet, I remain empty." The wise man replied, "That is because you have chosen the easy course. Anyone can travel around and endure physical discomfort. Take the truly brave trip. Travel through yourself."

244. The real intelligence of an individual can be measured by the number of things from which he need not escape. A cosmically mature man does not need to escape the consequences of foolish acts, for he performs none. He need not escape from social enemies because he dwells above the level of human conflict and hostility. Anyone not living in a jungle has no need to escape wolves or foxes or anything else. Read this paragraph again.

245. Be authentic. That is your entire satisfaction. In a small shop in Germany a skilled craftsman made violins of magnificent quality. He produced only a few violins each year, which were eagerly purchased by those who appreciated quality. Hearing about the violins, a large factory began to manufacture thousands of imitations, which were inferior in every way. The skilled craftsman knew about the imitations, but remained satisfied with the knowledge that his products were the original and the authentic.

246. A man living outside the circle of delusion which imprisons most men has a question of everyone he meets. Usually asked silently, the question is, "Can you get outside of yourself for even a split second in order to hear something you have never heard before?" Those who learn to hear will enter a new world.

247. An American vessel left a port in Massachusetts to head for a distant shore where the crew was

instructed to find specimens of rare tropical fruits. The journey took four months. When landing, the crew took only fifteen minutes to collect the plants they wanted. A person may work inwardly for a long time without seeing any sign of self-elevation. But if the necessary voyage has been taken, he will someday find himself surrounded by bright rewards.

248. Said someone, "I am trying to understand what is meant by an awakened man. What does he do?" Answer: "Think of what an awakened man does *not* do. He does not go around causing confusion and heartache while calling it social reform, as sleeping men do. He does not spread gloom and nervousness as others do. Few people know and appreciate his contribution, for only a whole mind can understand another whole mind."

249. A girl grew up in an isolated seacoast village which was usually covered with heavy fogs and mists. The girl was told about an inland village which had clear skies. But since wet weather was all she had known she had difficulty conceiving a fog-free place. But one week she traveled with her parents to the sunny town where she experienced its clear weather for herself. Many men and women remain in spiritual fog because they wrongly assume that fog is all that exists. The fact is, a clear land exists.

250. Man's condition is easily described by saying that he dwells in a state of deep psychic sleep. As proof of his sleep he would be horrified at the thought of spending several months on a brutal battlefield, yet he never wonders about his internal warfare which wounds him year after year. Sleeper, awake!

251. You can help yourself only by hearing cosmic wisdom. You can hear cosmic wisdom only from

someone who has it. You will find this person who has it by first eliminating all those who really do not have it. How can you know who does not have it? Listen to him. Listen with your cosmic mind. You will know, for a cracked bell sounds cracked.

252. A student from Scotland asked, "Why is it so difficult to talk someone out of persistent foolish behavior?" Came the reply, "Try to talk a flood out of flooding. It cannot be done because a flood is not conscious, it cannot hear. A human mind flooded with dark emotions will hear only dark emotions."

253. Say to yourself, "I have certain attitudes and ambitions. I also have friends and allies in these attitudes. But what would happen to me if they suddenly withdrew their support of me?" Do this and you will understand one kind of fear—the fear of standing all alone. But you *can* stand all alone, which is the only stand having no fear. Stand in the light of your own lamp and see for yourself. Self-discovery is really a lot of fun.

254. A lost human being accidentally attended a truth-talk. Because truth is hard on egotism the man silently and in hostility asked the speaker, "Who are you to tell me what to do?" The man's closed mind was unaware of the reply he might have heard: "I am someone who knows how much you suffer from being yourself. I am also someone who can help you escape yourself."

255. An earnest seeker found a piece of truth about the size of a walnut. He showed it to various groups of people to see what they would do with it. A group of neighbors showed no interest, believing it to simply be a dull object of some kind. A religious group feared

it, declaring it to be the product of evil forces. Some businessmen wanted to advertise and commercialize it. The owner finally decided to show it only to those who wanted to find their own piece of truth.

256. A study of human gullibility is essential, for gullibility and danger go together. A sheep in alliance with a wolf against other sheep foolishly thinks it lessens the wolf's appetite toward himself. Gullibility accounts for half the shocks received by any individual in daily life. Inner light banishes gullibility.

257. A mother was teaching her daughter to bake bread. Misunderstanding instructions, the daughter placed a dozen unneeded ingredients on the table. Seeing the clutter, the mother directed, "Get the wrong ones out of the way." That is also a basic principle for self-change. Self-examination reveals our actual attitudes, after which we can get the wrong ones out of the way.

258. A student in class raised his hand to request, "Please motivate us to transform our ways of thinking." The teacher instructed, "Think how often you have been painfully stuck with the choices you made. Now ask whether you want to retain the kind of mind that made these harmful decisions."

259. Said a teacher during an informal discussion, "You accept certain answers as being the right answers. Look carefully at your day and tell me the results of living from these answers. I speak about inward results. Do your answers allow you to pass freely through your day, or do they fail you? If failing, does it make sense to cling to them? Reject your usual answers, just as you refuse the wrong tools for repairing a lamp. There is an Answer."

260. If you are disappointed by pleasures that vanish overnight, walk the inner path. It is the only real pleasure to be found on earth. Others know this unique pleasure, and so can you know it. It is as pleasurable as walking away from the noises of a big city to enter the quietness of the woods.

WHY A TRANSFORMED MIND IS ESSENTIAL

261. An original copy of the British Magna Carta fell into the hands of a tailor who did not know its value. He was just about to cut it into measuring strips when it was rescued by a caller who recognized its historical importance. Because man does not recognize the practical value of truth he snips it to suit his own shallow purposes. A transformed mind is necessary.

262. Something within you is able to hear truth when it sends its message of rescue. Nothing can prevent this, not past mistakes, not feelings of hopelessness, not another person. So awaken this higher hearing, then, the message will come, just as you hear a distant bell above the noise of your surroundings.

263. Several men and women had an opportunity to watch an expert sculptor at work. One man, a frustrated sculptor, sat there in silent envy and scorn. A woman who had just quarreled with her husband expressed anger toward the sculptor because he was also a man. Other observers had equally negative attitudes. Consequently, none could either enjoy the sculptor's work or learn from it. Human beings block their own opportunity to learn from an expert in cosmic consciousness. Grow inwardly rich by rising above such pettiness.

264. A teacher was noted for his direct advice. One day a seeker asked for help. The teacher came right to the point by replying, "To be helped we must want help more than we want to hide things from ourselves." Be helped by this lesson.

265. Suppose you see a real diamond and an artificial diamond side by side on a table. If you want the real diamond you must learn how to distinguish between the two. You must not assume that you already know the difference. The inner work you are now doing will enable you to tell the difference between real and unreal teachings. True power and pleasure will then be yours.

266. A class heard, "You live in anxiety because you fail to see that a thought is only a thought. You think something will be lost by missing your favorite television program. What really bothers you is the interruption of your regular routine, for it provides a feeling of security, a false feeling. The interruption suddenly leaves you with nothing to do, with no expectations, which is frightening to the conditioned mind. Drop the thought that you can lose something and there is nothing to lose."

267. A teacher of pure truth stood before a class of new students. "Each of you," he said, "has a part which wants inner light, but you also have a part which prefers to remain in darkness. Listen carefully. Only the right part of you is admitted to this class. The insincere part must be left outside. There will be no compromise between the two parts. Do you understand?" Sensing the teacher's cosmic power, the students nodded.

268. A man knows not what he does to himself. He would never dream of behaving badly toward the king of his country, yet constantly displays disrespectful manners toward the inner king which consists of his own real nature. Man knows not what he does to himself. You can be different. You can treat yourself with courtesy.

269. I will tell you of an extremely intelligent statement to make. Declare, "I am not going to do this to myself any more." This is said by one who realizes at last that he is his own worst enemy, that defeat and distress is punishment on himself by himself. He is like a businessman who criticizes a faulty financial report, only to discover it was his own. But his humiliation turns to inspiration by declaring, "I am not going to do this to myself any more." Nothing is more intelligent than honest self-correction.

270. Suppose you believe you understand your own nature, but really do not. Suppose you assume you are using your mind at full capacity, but are not doing so. See what the dropping of the belief and the assumption will do for you? New knowledge refreshes, like discovering a stream in a dry land.

271. Two men stood on a wharf, watching incoming ships. One of them soon lost interest and walked away. The other man kept watching for anything of interest, which soon appeared. One ship was flying a special flag which indicated it had found buried treasure. That was of great interest to him. Cosmically, anyone interested in seeing something will eventually see something which interests him—like ways to refuse intimidation from other people.

272. Imagine yourself with outstretched hands in the darkness of your home as you grope toward a lamp. With relief you finally feel something solid. There is no better illustration of what finally happens to those who persist in spite of the darkness. They finally feel something quite solid. It is called True Power.

273. "Please tell us about something we do not as yet know," requested a class member. The teacher answered, "You do not as yet know of another viewpoint you can have toward yourself, toward other people, toward daily life. This is a supreme viewpoint, having none of the pettiness of usual viewpoints. This supreme viewpoint frees you of surrounding storms, just as the moon sails serenely through dark clouds."

274. Life for most people is an odd and fickle dream. There is a way to awaken. Look at it in the following way. You have an undeveloped region within. With more knowledge and application this region can be developed. You then stand in a new place of commanding comprehension. Do not lose the profound message in these few words because of their simplicity. Study and apply them.

275. Man's mind is like a whirlpool that agitates and distorts everything falling into it. He takes dependency as loyalty, cunning as intelligence, gullibility as cooperation. When will he learn better? When he makes up his mind to no longer go along with a world that calls nonsense sense. There is a higher world for you.

276. Suppose you enter a zoo with the pleasant anticipation of viewing interesting animals from faraway places. But inside the animal areas you see no animals at all. Instead, there are signs which merely describe

camels and leopards and elephants. You would be disappointed at seeing words instead of actualities. Man remains disappointed because he knows only the descriptions of love and understanding. You can know and live the actual states.

277. A man who had applied himself diligently to the inner adventure told some other seeker, "There is one thing I definitely know now that I did not know before. I know that inner strength keeps *me* going well when exterior *events* do not go well."

278. Picture in your mind a squad of ten weary soldiers. One takes command for a moment, ordering the others to march west. Then a second and a third and a fourth soldier take over to command the others to march east, north, south. That illustrates the wrong operation of a human mind. The soldiers are dictatorial and contradictory thoughts which force a man to march pointlessly, wearing him out. Everyone has had this personal experience. Your present studies will change this, producing a mind having a single commander, which is higher consciousness.

279. A student asked his teacher, "Why does the truth hurt?" Reply: "Speaking generally you can say that it is the truth that hurts, but more specifically it is our refusal of truth that causes pain. Suppose a man accepts the fact that he is deceitful. Now he is no longer in painful conflict with that fact. Also, his self-honesty begins to work on deceit to end it."

280. The religion or philosophy a man really believes in is the one he lives out with his daily actions and attitudes, whether open or secret. A fox who has learned to bleat like a sheep will still behave like a fox. This fact protects you from human foxes.

THE PATH TO TRUE SECURITY

281. Said a student to the teacher, "You say that our securities are illusory, and that we must see them as false. This would be valuable, but how can we see it?" Answer: "By daring to see it. How would you feel if someone close to you left you? Honestly concede that you would be hurt and angry. That is a valuable admission of living in artificial security. Know this. When able to understand an event before it happens, there will be no pain in you if it happens."

282. Humanity is like a group of passengers on a ship, attending a noisy party, not realizing that the ship is lost and drifting. The great spiritual teachers of history have urged, "See what is happening. The course can be corrected if only you will see what is happening." But the party goes on. But you can correct your own course.

283. Your aim is to know who you are *from yourself*. Few people know who they are from individual self-knowledge. Most people have vague assumptions about their identities which come from other people, from diplomas, marriage, financial and social success, and from assorted labels and titles. Members of a class in South Carolina spent an entire month discovering who they were not. First discover who you are not, for then you will know who you are *from yourself*. Now you are out of the human jungle.

284. Stay uninvolved. Learn the wisdom of remaining uninvolved. Stay uninvolved with the offending remark or the disappointing event, with the activity offering nothing more than temporary stimulation. You have a much greater mission—involvement with finding Real

Life. A man digging a well pays no attention to nearby children playing games. He wants water.

285. The difference between those who don't talk and those who do can be illustrated. A king sent ten soldiers to explore a strange and distant land which was said to contain great wealth and beauty. Nine of the soldiers stood at a distance and studied the land through binoculars. Then they gave long and complicated lectures about the land they had never visited. But the tenth soldier walked the very hills of the unfamiliar country. Returning, he gave the king a beautiful stone he had collected. "This single stone," declared the pleased king, "is worth a thousand lectures."

286. People love to delude themselves into thinking that mere action can change the human condition, such as political or social action. The action of a charging bull also changes many things. The only action capable of changing the human condition from lower to higher is the action which raises the level of a mind's consciousness. You are now entering this new kind of action.

287. A teacher asked his class, "How can a person grow much faster?" One perceptive student replied, "We grow much faster by having no need to have others know that we know."

288. Why don't you let Truth work for you? That is what Truth is for. Why continue with strained and useless labor? But a connection must be made between you and energetic Truth. That connection is affection. One member of a study group turned his affection toward the reading of books which provided blunt but healthy information. He made the connection. Make your own.

289. A disciple of a great teacher was asked, "How do you know that your teacher really knows?" Replied the disciple, "By a thousand small signs. I will tell you of one I have witnessed many times. He is asked many foolish and insincere questions by self-deceived people. Only an exceedingly perceptive mind knows enough to not answer the questions as if they have sincerity or merit."

290. Of all the strange moves by man, none is stranger than self-justification. Justification of a foolish or harmful act perpetuates the self-punishment residing in that act. Self-justification becomes an inner judge who condemns the foolish person to continue to live with his own wretchedness. Self-honesty is the cure.

291. As a class experiment in the power of the human voice, some college students placed themselves at ten different levels on a mountain slope. They found, for example, that a shout from the peak of the mountain could be heard only by those on the two levels immediately below. This illustrates a cosmic law: Men with higher consciousness can reach only those who have climbed within hearing distance. Such climbers can understand. Those on lower levels may assume they understand cosmic facts, but their quarrels and depressions say otherwise. Climb within hearing distance.

292. Man has everything needed for self-transformation. His first step is awareness, no matter how dim, of his unique ability to rise above his present level. His second step is to take enthusiastic responsibility for personal advancement. A child is given the cardboard letters of the alphabet, but he must make personal effort to set them in the right order.

293. A certain realization brought inner victory to one man. He realized that mere opinions are highly popular with lazy minds because they can be possessed without effort. Unafraid of mental effort, he replaced stale opinions with self-transforming information. Use this secret for peaceful human relations.

294. A new student was still in the immature stage where he preferred arguing to learning. One day the teacher remarked to him casually, "It's your life— do whatever you want with it." The unexpected statement helped the pupil. The teacher's attitude of dismissal shattered the student's egotistical belief that he was needed by the teacher. Also, it threw the pupil back on himself to reveal how little command he really had.

295. Someone obeying the laws of the land may be quite unaware of how he breaks the laws of his own nature. His chief problem is failure to realize that he does in fact live within a system of natural laws. The following bright news can help him to become a happier citizen inwardly: All natural laws operate for his benefit, not for his restriction. A bird sings freely and naturally because it is what it is. It does not try to imitate a violin.

296. What causes human frustration? It is caused by an attempt to make conditioned thought do work it cannot do. Someone believes that joining a club or cause will banish boredom and loneliness, so he acts on that belief. His pain will remain. An automobile cannot fly like an airplane. Only a conscious mind, not a conditioned mind, possesses liberty from every frustration.

297. A student helped his classmates by saying, "I realize why we are here in class. Let me state the problem. Man has a dreadful talent for appearing good on

the outside while being the exact opposite inwardly. When this occurs we say he is self-divided or that he is a hypocrite. We are here to make the inner and the outer the same, which is sanity and decency."

298. Envy of other people's supposed happiness or success is like envying someone who owns an artificial diamond. We approach a bit closer to our own happiness by realizing that other people are not nearly as happy or confident as they appear to be.

299. Do not hope for a brilliant flash of light from heaven to suddenly illuminate your world. It does not happen that way. Prefer the practical to the sensational. Only the patient and cheerful gathering of practical points can supply the desired illumination. It can be accurately described as that small but definite glow you see when approaching the exit of a dark tunnel.

300. Some camels decided to hold a beauty contest. All the animals of desert and forest were invited to participate. Many attractive entrants appeared, including elk, lion and zebra. When the camel judges made their decisions, all five prizes went to camels. When the other animals protested, the chief camel advised, "Your complaint is invalid on two counts. Firstly, the judges were selected for their fairness, honesty and impartiality. Secondly, as you should know, only camels are competent judges of beauty."

HOW OTHER SEEKERS
HAVE SUCCEEDED

301. Asked a student, "How have others succeeded?" Answered the teacher, "Every person who has succeeded in the inner quest did so by passing a certain kind of test. The test was a willingness to bear uncertainty, to

permit the winds of Reality to blow away his carefully constructed psychological securities. Then, on the bare ground, he saw the creation of something truly certain."

302. Never pause along the path for anything, not to hide from a frightening fact, not to listen to attractive but false voices. Always move on, even though you have no idea of where you are going. By the way, you are going to a land as high above earth as the stars, where no other person can ever become a problem to you.

303. You should reject falsehood because it is false to *you*. Think with depth upon this idea and you will see where you have been loyal to a traitor. It is as if a soldier at your side suddenly reveals himself to be one of the enemy. Truth delivers what falsehood can only slyly promise to deliver. Let truth deliver a new life to you.

304. There is a psychic law regarding the use of one's own resources which must be pondered endlessly. It was once stated at a lecture, "The man who knocks his house apart is the only man who can put it together again."

305. A class in Wales reached the period for open discussion. The teacher supplied the topic, "The unnatural self always distorts the truth, while the natural self cannot distort it. So if feeling the conflict of distortion we know what is causing it. What are your comments?" A student responded, "Our task is to end the tyranny of unnaturalness."

306. When a person plays a dramatic and impressive role he anxiously hopes that you will believe in it. If you do, both you and the actor gain nothing. The psychic actor can be encouraged to drop his role to

become a real person by your polite and quiet refusal to see him as he wrongly sees himself. So your trueness is a high level of virtue and morality that helps everyone, just as sunshine dissolves dampness in every yard.

307. Needed knowledge is available, fully available, but one must become personally involved with it. The collecting process can be compared with someone standing in a shallow stream while gazing downward at various stones. He becomes personally involved by reaching down through the water to pick up a particular stone. Do you know when one is really having a personal involvement with truth? When one feels he has picked up something strangely different, something having a new kind of attraction.

308. A man of real knowledge told his listeners, "Human beings remain in their psychic beds, sleeping their lives away, never knowing what they are missing. They sleep without knowing they are asleep. I tell you that your fear and your suffering are unnecessary. Wake up!"

309. A motorist wanted to reach home before a storm broke. He found himself in unfamiliar territory, but believed he knew the right road home. But he paused a moment to ask himself the very intelligent question, "Is it possible that I am self-deceived?" A check of a map corrected his route, which led him home safely. Every human being on the road of life should ask the supremely intelligent question, "Is it possible that I am self-deceived?"

310. A father was helping his son to build a model ship. Running into a difficulty, the boy complained, "These parts bother me." Handing the boy the page of

instructions, the father replied, "What really bothers you is what you don't know." That is also what bothers us when trying to build a right life. But what we don't know can be known. Know human nature, and half your problems will end.

311. Anyone locked inside wrong attitudes toward himself and toward life cannot conceive of anything outside of himself. He is as confined as a room without windows. He cannot see anything but his old and boring surroundings. Almost all attempts to call him out to play will be ignored or battled. Happily, those with a yearning to break out can do so. Those who made it to the outside were aided by an astonishing fact. They observed and were amazed at their own strange fondness for self-confinement.

312. If you persist as others have persisted, you will observe what they have observed. You will see quite clearly the falling away of a worry or a compulsion or a tension. It will fall away like an arrow at the end of its flight. It will fall because in your new consciousness you no longer supply it with power for flight.

313. Society is far from being what it tries so hard to appear to be. What is praised as friendliness or as the cheerful sharing of social responsibilities is usually nothing more than the fear of being alone. A grounded airplane can make a lot of noise, but that noise is not flight. So this Path to Reality is for those unafraid to see beyond surface appearances, both in themselves and others. They are the real winners in life.

314. The Italian painter Raphael once worked in a room having a large overhead dome which admitted a single bright light. Books can serve a similar purpose. Keep yourself under the bright light of truthful books. It changes you, which changes conditions.

315. Said a class member, "I have several conflict-ing feelings toward someone close to me who rejects self-development. I probably have false guilt about it. Please comment." The member heard, "If he chooses to dwell in self-defeating hostility to truth, it is his tragedy and his responsibility. It is not your tragedy or responsibility, and could not be even if you wished them to be. The cosmic law of personal responsibility can-not be broken. Your own rightness will show you how to think and act toward him."

316. Picture two tape recorders facing each other on a table, both loudly playing human chatter. That is society's idea of effective human communication. Real communication exists on a much higher level in which two people have at least some capacity for mental silence. Their relationship will be enjoyable.

317. Someone asked, "Why is a free man free?" Reply: "Because he knows something you do not know. He knows he does not exist in the false sense that unfree people think they exist. Therefore, he has neither the pains nor confusions that go with a false existence. He has the freedom of a former actor who has removed his costume and is therefore no longer a slave to the audience."

318. Not understanding himself, man also fails to understand the warring society he has created. He is like a child who drops a toy and then wonders why it breaks. Society gets smashed because it consists of hypnotized human beings who dream they are awake. The truly awakened ones look out at society with comprehension. They put two and two together and get four, not five or six.

319. What imagination sees is not what a Whole Mind sees. Impress yourself with this fact by saying, "What is seen by imagination is not all there is. There is something higher." Whoever does not imagine himself a victim cannot be a victim. When the imaginary self melts, so does both victim and persecutor. Man hides like a hunted animal, not seeing that the hunter is really his unconscious self. See beyond imagination. There is something higher.

320. "There is one thing I know," an inquirer told a teacher of cosmic facts. "I know how helpless I feel in this strange world." Replied the teacher, "I will tell you something you may not know. There is something within you that is stronger than the world."

THE STORY OF A UNIQUE KING

321. A dictator of ancient Crete was riding through the streets with his guard when a scene caught his attention. A plainly dressed philosopher was speaking to a crowd which showed a deep interest in the message. The dictator asked a stranger at the edge of the crowd, "Who is that man?" The stranger replied, "He is a king." The alarmed dictator asked, "Over what kingdom does he reign?" Said the stranger, "Over himself."

322. Imagine a man trying to lead himself out of a dangerous jungle by taking his own hand. That is what happens when a desperate person relies on conditioned thoughts for his deliverance. Something outside of his habitual ideas must take his hand. Whether it is called God or Truth or Cosmic Consciousness, it is ready to reach out toward those who reach toward it. Reach today.

323. Psychic silver appears to whoever takes full and personal responsibility for his wrong decisions. A wrong decision is one that hurts that right part of you that wants to walk away from society's furor. It is a wrong decision to believe that social confusion has power over you. You have power over yourself, but may not know it. One day this power will make negative states retreat like a beaten army. The victory starts by taking full and personal responsibility for wrong decisions.

324. A disciple praised his teacher, "What an inspiring lecture you gave today! Hundreds were thrilled." Sighed the teacher, "Ah, yes, but wait until tomorrow. They will hardly remember having been here. The noise of the daily world will block recollection of the inspiration which could create a new world."

325. A demon disguised himself as a truth-teacher. Able to repeat the truth mechanically, he soon gathered a large following. Observing all this, the demon's cousin felt alarmed. "Is this not hazardous?" he asked the teaching demon. "What if they sense the real meaning behind your words?" The teaching demon laughed, "You don't understand. The first thing they asked me was whether they could have a feeling of importance by joining the organization. When I smilingly nodded they practically worshipped me. Have no fears, cousin." It is important only to be real.

326. A teacher explained, "Stupidity is easily defined. It is a state in which one does not know that which he proudly assumes he knows. So stupidity includes vanity, self-deception, and worst of all, a hardened mind unable to receive anything really new. Trying to reason with anyone in this condition is like trying to teach English to an ox." Awareness of ignorance erases ignorance.

327. A woman who owned a real estate company told the class, "We must make the invisible bars visible. Take the painful feeling that you do more work than others but receive less pay and appreciation. Many prisoners are crowded behind these bars without knowing it. We can either suffer from them or break out through higher understanding. We are here to break out. Let's get on with it."

328. Truth is enough. Remember that. Truth is all you need. Just as there is one sky which covers everything on earth, so is there one vast truth which covers all your needs. This is inspiration, but is also practical fact. Truth is enough.

329. A student asked a question about conflict. The teacher replied, "Strange man invites conflicts into his life because without them his days would seem dull and meaningless. Strife provides a false feeling of life, an unhealthy thrill. Man must voluntarily surrender these false excitements before life can have real purpose and meaning. This profound fact is seldom realized by men, but is pondered deeply by those who want out."

330. A small child stood at the bottom of some steps to look up at his father who stood at the top of the stairs. The child pleaded for his parent's help in climbing up. Said the father, "Climb the first three steps for yourself, then I will help you." By self-effort we earn the right to higher help.

331. A certain man was known for his foolishness. One day he announced his intention of traveling through a dark and dangerous wilderness while carrying only his favorite walking stick. A friend warned, "But it is foolish to enter there without a torch." The man smiled in a superior manner. "You don't understand," he said. "See

this stick? I intend to *call it a torch!"* Foolish men mistake words for realities, then complain of their falls.

332. If a jeweler's display case is heaped high with old newspapers he will have no room for his precious stones. And if our minds are filled with pointless and repetitious thoughts, we have no room for valuable thinking. Make room for cosmic gems.

333. There is a certain point at which a seeker may stop his own progress. It can be called the anger-point. The anger-point is reached when a presented truth requests a hearer to abandon cherished falsehood in favor of fresh fact. Both anger and fear are there, though the hearer may be quite clever in concealing them. Anger-points decrease by having a strong preference for self-advancement over so-called self-protection. We must be like young eagles who dare to leave the nest because they have sighted the vast world beyond.

334. It is cosmic law that one must pay for anything worthwhile. Payment might consist of recognizing a vanity, of exploring a new idea, of dropping dependency. Help yourself to make payment by remembering that the bait in a trap is always free.

335. A member of the audience requested of the speaker, "May we hear about genuine compassion?" The speaker replied, "Suppose you learn your lessons well. In time you will dissolve personal anguish, which means you no longer see it as necessary to yourself. You can now also see pain as unnecessary for others, so you help them as you helped yourself, like a self-cured physician who cures others. This is genuine compassion."

336. A girl found a seed of unusual appearance. Acting on her wonder about the seed, she planted it.

The seed produced a colorful flower. Do you have an attractive wonder about these teachings? That wonder is the seed of new life. Let it develop as it wishes. Real power and pleasure will result.

337. A small shop was located on an obscure street in a large city. Only one product was on display, which was a small box labeled *New Mind*. The shopkeeper explained to those who entered, "I have but one product to sell, which is why I have so few customers. Most people patronize shops selling wealth and popularity. However, my product is composed of quality ingredients which succeed for all who want a new mind. I urge you to try it."

338. A class was told, "You are trying to live a vitalized life by following the example of bewildered society. That is like trying to draw a deer while using a bull as a model. All will be distorted. This is easily proven by noticing the kind of results you get from the model you use."

339. When making a mistake of any kind it is vital to not build a second mistake on top of it. It would be a second mistake to fall into mechanical emotions over an error, such as condemning yourself or feeling bitter toward those who victimized you. Such reactions pin you down to the very level of mechanical behavior which causes mistakes. Instead, refuse to go along with your usual reactions. Try to see how unclear thinking causes the error. This separates you from mistakes, just as you might depart from an angry and dangerous mob.

340. Suppose an explorer was about to enter a new and beautiful land. But suppose he paused at its entrance to demand, "Now, then, I wish to see a sparkling lake at my right, also, I wish to view a large grove of oak

trees." That would ruin everything, for his demand would clash with the natural unfolding of the land. Do we experience daily conflict because of similar demands?

THE POWER OF SELF-COMPLETION

341. Man in his present state is incomplete, like a half-finished cathedral. So the aim of life is self-completion. Once attained, the noise and confusion that accompanies construction is heard no more. So if you are tired of psychic noise, complete yourself. Then, you will no longer fear anyone or anything.

342. We interpret things according to our level of understanding—or misunderstanding. A small boy was taken to an outdoor concert by his mother. A famous soprano was part of the program. On the way home the boy asked, "Why was that man shaking a stick at that woman?" His mother replied, "That was the conductor and he was not shaking a stick at her." The boy persisted, "Then why was she screaming?" View the whole picture, not just one small corner.

343. Self-transformation is a process of subtraction. We must subtract the unnatural. It starts with detection. We can detect strained behavior or mechanical talking. Subtract the artificial and the real remains naturally, just as a stream flows casually in the absence of rocks.

344. The owner of a wild horse wished to make it gentle and peaceful. Hearing of a famous horse tamer he brought the animal over to the trainer's ranch. He was about to knock on the door when he noticed something peculiar about the horses belonging to the famous trainer. All were wild and hostile. Sensing something wrong, he returned home at once. He told his wife, "Never hire a horse tamer without looking around."

345. Imagine someone wildly tossing stones on a dark night. He pretends to know who and what they will strike, but not really knowing, he fears the consequences. This describes mistake-making man. His errors and resulting punishments appear because of his unconsciousness—which he calls intelligence. So what makes more sense than to seek and dwell in mental light?

346. Here is a method used by one man for inner advancement. He realized that the right combination of several ideas would create a wholeness of understanding, just as many colors create a whole rainbow. So by connecting the idea of resentment with self-punishment, he knew he could have nothing to do with resentment. By connecting the idea of self-knowledge with the idea of true confidence, he felt inspired to gain more self-knowledge.

347. It is easier to criticize the weeds in a neighbor's yard than to rid one's own yard of weeds. This is how people live, then complain that they are not surrounded by flowers!

348. One after another the members of an audience spoke of their various problems to the teacher. He replied, "One answer will cover every difficulty mentioned. I will supply the solution, after which you must ponder the words deeply." Everyone listened attentively as the teacher stated, "The answer dwells in the mind's silence, not in its agitated activities."

349. Man is most incredibly ignorant when he tries to separate the painful results in his day from his own nature which produced those results. As if the quality of the table can be separated from the table-maker!

350. Have you ever wondered how on earth you can change yourself and your life—*really* change them?

I will show you how. Stop trying to think your way to a change. It never works, as you well know. Instead, take a leap, yes, much as you might leap across a stream. Leave the familiar shore to find yourself in mid-air. *It is the mid-air experience that changes you.* Forget both the old shore and the new shore; just take the leap.

351. An elderly couple were on vacation when distressing news arrived. Their home had been damaged by a storm. They felt depressed at the thought of returning to the uncomfortable home. But their sadness was unnecessary, for their wealthy son had turned a new home over to them. Man wrongly believes he must return daily to the self-damage of irritation and confusion and tension. Not at all. Self-newness has been provided for all who will accept it.

352. A study group in London was discussing the damage done by human pretense. Someone volunteered the information, "If there were no other reason for giving up pretense, the burden it imposes on the pretender would be reason enough." That was sharp thinking.

353. A sheep who felt neglected carelessly fell into a ditch. To his surprise he felt a new importance as the rescuing sheep bleated out their sympathies toward him. From that day forward he fell into ditches regularly, always receiving sympathetic rescue. He noticed something about his rescuers. They would get nervous and even show irritation toward the careless sheep when he delayed his fall too long. Study this strange fact about human nature.

354. It is an interesting paradox. Here is someone who is at last approaching a self-fact he has been avoiding for years. The closer he comes the more it scares him, but at the same time he senses the increasing

presence of practical knowledge for handling the fact. Seeing his actual hostility for the first time, his fear fades before comprehension. Realizing the danger of hiding a leopard in the cellar, he goes into practical action to get rid of it. One action he takes is to cease to enjoy the unnatural pleasure in hostility.

355. Once when the opera *Aida* was about to be performed a singer was missing. Frantically, the manager searched around for a substitute, but none could be found. There was only one thing the manager could do, so he did it. He sang the role himself. Sooner or later we must stop depending upon others, and must personally do what must be done for ourselves. That builds inner strength.

356. "At one of our classes," a student said, "you made a comment that came home with me. You said that a man can have a ton of education without having an ounce of intelligence. It is clearer to me that real intelligence is a result of self-knowledge, not knowledge of science or history or religion."

357. A visitor to some botanical gardens was interested in rare flowers. She was sighted by a male employee of the gardens who wished to tell her about a new section of rare flowers, but the woman suddenly disappeared in the crowd. She returned home not knowing what she had missed that day. Millions of human beings live without realizing they have missed the prize that could be theirs. You can win the prize of pleasant human relations.

358. Be pleased at the number of good things you can do for yourself. You can make the inner person and the outer person the same. You can realize that the art of self-healing is known and practiced perfectly by an

inner center you can develop. You can remain at ease in any situation which now causes nervousness. You can rely on cosmic sight for understanding any condition at a glance, which is like finding binoculars when needing them.

359. Asked a student, "Why do people shun authentic teachers who could show them the way out?" The group-leader explained, "It is like an actor so fond of his stage role that he shuns everyone except those who applaud his dramatic performance. The insecure actor fears being caught out of his role. But beyond the role is the real. True security, founded on the rock of cosmic knowledge, is unshakable."

360. If you really want out of the human jungle I will show you how to stop wasting time. When with a group or an individual offering help, listen very carefully to the topics of the speeches and conversations. Then, on the way home ask yourself, "Do these topics connect with internal change, which alone can help me?" If there is no connection, there is nothing for you there. This method enables you to distinguish between practical and useless counsel, just as you sort the day's mail into the important and the trivial.

INTERESTING FACTS ABOUT SELF-VALUE

361. Said a king to a wise man, "I wish to be valuable to my people. Please show me how." Replied the wise man, "First be valuable to yourself. This avoids self-deception. You see, the less value a man has for himself the more he believes he can contribute benefits to others. This brings injury to both. To give gold you must have gold."

362. Man is like a clock with abundant energy but whose hands run backward. Here is how anyone can correct the direction of his day. The next time you are disappointed by something, ask why your mind chose the reaction of disappointment. That reaction is not necessary. You can always choose to understand an event, and that understanding will contain no disappointment.

363. Here is how one woman cured herself of suppressed resentment. First she saw how resentment was caused by her own artificial attitudes. For example, she pretended to care for certain people for whom she really cared nothing. These people took advantage of her, which she resented. She then dropped her artificiality, which ended her involvement with the people and ended her resentment.

364. A spiritual guide taught his class, "You want to change your life without changing yourself. Impossible. You *are* your life. You and your life are the very same thing. This can be understood with the illustration of ground for planting crops. Healthy soil produces good crops, while inferior ground can only produce worthless harvests. The nature of the ground and the nature of the crops cannot be separated. Neither can your nature be separated from the results of that nature. So self-change alone creates life-change."

365. Scientists finally noticed the connection between the moon and the tides. This was practical knowledge for men on ship and shore. Make inner connections. They are extremely practical. Can you see the connection between the way you act and the way you feel? Try. You will feel better about everything.

366. Some people heard about a collector of rare and health-giving herbs who lived in a cabin on a

mountain ridge. Interested in herbs, they ascended the mountain but found no one at the cabin. Then with binoculars they saw the collector several miles away, walking slowly toward them. Impatient at his leisurely approach, some of the people departed, so only the patient ones learned about the health-giving herbs. The lesson is that truth approaches us at its own wise pace. Our part is patient watching and waiting.

367. A seeker finally found what he sought. In teaching others he said, "The path to wisdom has three stages. A foolish man never doubts himself. A foolish man learning to be wise doubts everything accepted as true. A wise man never doubts himself."

368. An early Spanish explorer of South America handed a map to one of his lieutenants. "Use this," instructed the commander, "to find a pass through the mountains." Glancing at the map, the lieutenant protested, "But this covers limited territory." The commander nodded. "I know. I want you to go beyond the map." Truth wants us to go beyond the familiar, beyond ourselves.

369. "The dawn is breaking," remarked one member of a study group, "for one fact is becoming increasingly clear to me. Here is what I mean. The attempt to escape a problem is precisely what keeps it going, while an attempt to understand it will end it."

370. A married couple were having a quiet and thoughtful discussion one evening at home. The husband related, "As a young man I used to enjoy stopping for a sidewalk chat with a neighbor down the street. I never knew much about him except that he was somewhat elderly. For years I never understood the attraction, but just the other day it struck me. He was one of those rare human beings who was able to keep himself out

of things. I mean, he never turned my comments into comments about himself."

371. Desperation over one's life is the perfect start for changing one's life. But the desperation must include a persistent wish for genuine self-change. Many desperate people who cry for help are like humbled passengers on a sinking ship who cease to be humble at the first sight of land.

372. How gullibly people trust the words of others, rarely bringing their own intelligence into the situation. A traveler wanted to know the way to Bagdad. Going to a sign-maker he requested, "Make me a sign that points toward Bagdad." Handing the traveler the finished sign the sign-maker wanted to know, "But how does this help you reach Bagdad?" The traveler exploded, "Foolish man! Does not your own sign plainly point the way?"

373. Whatever is right within us is covered over by whatever is wrong, like a single red rose in a field of gray weeds. So the question is not, "Is there a rose there?" The question is, "Why do you tolerate all those weeds?"

374. Said a member of a group, "I will tell you why attendance here is essential to me. My chief problem is my inability to take care of myself properly from day to day. I mean, I never know just where I will impulsively act against myself." The member paused to ask the others, "Do you understand what I mean?" When the others nodded the member concluded, "Knowing myself a bit better, I am less and less acting against myself."

375. Consider this question: Why are human beings unable to see that self-deceived planners of a better

society can only make things worse? When this was discussed in a class a member volunteered, "There is one thing you can say for those who meet to plan peace and brotherhood for all. Sooner or later they will have a fight." There is a better way—called inner awakening.

376. Human help is like a man without a watch assuring everyone he can supply the right time. A class or lecture presenting authentic help is a rarity. It is so rare that visitors to a real class are unaware of being in a different kind of place. They always think or say the same thing, such as, "I have heard all this before in other classes." Others assume, "Oh, I see, this is another self-improvement group." It is nothing of the sort. For those who can see, it is a profound way to exchange old life for New Life.

377. If you hand a man a lemon and tell him that its sourness lies outside the lemon he will think you are joking. Yet with a perfectly straight face that same man will tell you that his sour life is caused by external events. When will man learn that he is the cause of his own feelings for either happiness or anxiety?

378. A skilled photographer comes up with good pictures because he can distinguish between an attractive scene and a dull one. We must distinguish between ordinary stimulation and cosmic inspiration. Winning a raise in pay or finding a new friend of the opposite sex provides stimulation, but not inspiration. Reading a truthful book or sensing the value of self-study provides inspiration, but not stimulation. Live with inspiration.

379. We can deceive ourselves and we can deceive others, but the truth cannot be deceived about anything. The truth does not knock unless there is somebody at home—and it always knows.

380. Troubled people assume that mental retreat from a raging world protects them from hurt and harm. That is like a careless man who believes he is locking a wolf outside his home when he is actually locking it in. Only conscious confrontation with the world can protect an individual. Eventually, to his astonishment, the individual sees he needed protection all right— but from himself.

HOW TO RECEIVE COSMIC KNOWLEDGE

381. Imagine an audience hearing a lecture by a man who really knows the truth about life. If you could see the invisible, here is what you would see. The speaker sends out rays of cosmic knowledge. Those already having at least a bit of knowledge pick up, respond to and appreciate the rays. Those without understanding are incapable of receiving the rays, therefore, they either ignore or reject what they hear. But the receptive ones are eager to hear more, for they know they have at last found the way.

382. The way out is found by those who constantly question their daily lives. One man advanced swiftly by asking himself, "What have my usual ways of thinking done for me? Have my habitual opinions and beliefs and attitudes provided the contentment I want? If not, it makes perfect sense for me to discover a new way of thinking and acting." This new way gives life real meaning.

383. A small child can make noise on a piano, but only an adult who understands the instrument can make music. Seek understanding of that marvelous instrument called the human mind.

384. Do not let other people interfere with what you must do for yourself. Under the spell of psychic hypnosis, and therefore not wanting rescue for themselves, they may try to discourage your efforts to break out. Be aware of their hostility toward truth, then quietly remove your mind from their influence. Be a Columbus on the psychic sea, letting no one stand in the way of your great discoveries.

385. A woman employed as a secretary said in class, "Last night a few of us discussed how lack of self-insight causes trouble. How does this apply in social relations?" Reply: "A man may be quite unaware of how he permits other people to use him for their personal advantages. He is unaware of this because he does the same thing; he exploits them. However, this fact is unacceptable to his flattering notion of himself as someone who is too noble to ever use others. So only self-honesty can end his exploitation by others."

386. Our own ways attract what we get from the world. A soldier wondered why his enemies never ran out of ammunition to fire at him. He then discovered he had carelessly left his own ammunition out in the open for his enemies to steal and use.

387. While relaxing under a tree on a hot and dry day, a man realized his need to travel to town on some business. But he had a strong yearning to remain in the comfortable shade. He declared, "I will let heaven make the decision. I will toss a stone at the tree. If it misses, I go. If it hits, I stay." So standing three feet from the tree, he threw the stone. When a man wants something, how coincidental that heaven's will and his will are the same.

388. Many people hesitate to seek the way out for fear it may not exist, but you must not do this, for the way out does exist. Anyone who declares, "I don't want to be lost in the woods any more," is already on his way out of the woods.

389. Confessed a newcomer in class, "My mind sometimes resembles a cage of wild animals. How can I tame them?" Answer: "Confine your mind to two areas. First, think sensibly toward your usual daily activities. Then spend the rest of your mental money on thoughts about your life here on earth and on how self-knowledge can make it a new life. Do that and your mind will come under self-control."

390. The real trouble with daydreaming is that it is so impractical. Some people have so many stars in their eyes they can't see one step ahead. This book is light along your path.

391. Many years ago a European merchant was viewed with wonder by his competitors. His cargo ships possessed a special wisdom for avoiding storms and for arriving in port ahead of schedule. Years later he revealed his secret. He had used trained pigeons to carry private information to him regarding weather and seas. Every person can develop his own private source of cosmic information which enables him to avoid psychic storms.

392. If you ever attend a class taught by a real teacher you should use the great opportunity wisely. For instance, be aware of your possible timidity when hearing new ideas, and do not let that timidity be a barrier to learning. Also, do not assume that you already understand a presented principle, for understanding is always a much deeper well than we imagine.

393. Worry is not part of your real nature. Worry is the result of unconscious and unnecessary submission to negative emotions. A man carried away by a raging river knows he is not a natural part of the river, so he swims for shore. Your natural wish to escape the emotional flood is evidence that a shore exists for you.

394. Both words and music are needed to complete a song. Both knowledge and inspiration are needed to make a whole human being. Knowledge comes first. Gather it with affection. Then you will know the difference between merely reading the words of the inner song and singing it.

395. Imagine a group of people standing on an ocean pier. One man falls into the water where he cries for help. All of the onlookers immediately pull out paper and pencils and begin to write essays on how to save a man struggling in the water. But along comes a sensible witness who throws down a life preserver which saves the man. Only an individual with cosmic consciousness can rescue struggling man. The others can only write and talk about it.

396. "Success will arrive," a teacher assured his class, "by seeing deeply into the short lesson I will now provide. Starting now, never mind how other people treat you. Instead, ask yourself how you treat yourself. The more it shocks you the more I congratulate you."

397. Some foxes met to declare, "If only we could learn to love each other more! So from this day forward we will use the word *love* in every sentence we use." Unfortunately, the repeated use of the word *love* had a peculiar and hypnotic effect on the foxes. They fell under the delusion that saying the word meant possession of the virtue. So they could never understand how such loving foxes could hate each other so much.

398. Do not feel that time is against self-awakening, for insight does not occur in man-made measurements of time. Each answer appears in the present moment of perception. So just as the wind does not recognize a tree as an obstacle, you need not recognize time as a barrier to self-illumination.

399. Australian engineers once changed the direction of a river, making it flow toward and serve the needs of a populated area. Do the same with your natural flow of alertness. Direct it toward needs, not toward trivialities. For instance, be alert toward your own misunderstanding, which can correct it, instead of judging the misunderstanding of other people. This is the flow of true wisdom.

400. The science of geology can tell you about the earth, and the science of oceanography can inform you of the seas, but only this Celestial Science can tell you about yourself. So let this higher science dominate your studies. It delivers real confidence.

THE FOUNDATIONS OF
REAL HAPPINESS

401. A teacher asked his class, "Have you recently heard anyone praise self-reliance? How long since you have observed someone who practices simplicity in daily living or who really places virtue before self-interest?" When the class remained silent the teacher stated, "Now you know why you live in such an unhappy world."

402. A master demon was instructing a student demon in the art of evil. "It is much easier to snare people than you may think," assured the master demon. "One of the best ways is to make them think that lies

are necessary to their psychic survival. They will believe this lie every time, but drive the delusion even deeper by showing them how to lie about their lies. For example, help them to justify their cruelties by saying they are only doing what was done to them. Being childish they will pounce on this gleefully, and they are yours."

403. A dove does not listen to the advice of a hawk, no matter how impressive the hawk may appear. The dove knows its own needs from its own nature. And you know what you need better than any other human being on earth. Your knowledge may not be conscious as yet, but it is there. To make it visible, trust yourself more than you trust anyone else. But trust the right part of you, the natural part which wants mental rebirth above all else.

404. It is easy to tell the difference between an ego-building belief and a self-liberating fact. A belief requires nervous protection by the believer, while a fact stands alone and unconcerned. There is no need to protect a page of print free of errors.

405. At a meeting a woman said, "During the day I forget things too easily. It is inconvenient." The teacher explained, "Forgetfulness is simply the inability to think about the right thing at the right time. You may forget your shopping list when leaving home because your mind is wandering off into worry over a family problem. You will learn here how to remain with yourself every moment, which corrects forgetfulness."

406. Man is frightened because he fails to understand higher causes, just as a small child might be puzzled at an airplane's passing shadow. Fear fades with the gathering of cosmic facts.

407. Four frightened men lived in different parts of the country. They were anxious because they did not know what to do with their lives. Each dawn was a new terror. By accident they happened to meet. With great joy they hit upon a solution to their purposeless lives. They formed an organization which specialized in telling other people what to do with their lives.

408. Human beings have great difficulty in seeing the lack of private merit in public ceremony. This is because they love ceremony more than merit. The excitement of public ceremony does nothing to end private anguish. A crown never cured a headache.

409. "The other day," a student stated to the teacher, "you gave us an interesting thought. You said we must do a different kind of thing with uncomfortable experiences. What was meant?" Said the teacher, "Most people either sullenly submit to uncomfortable experiences or they openly rebel. You must do something different. You must study yourself to see why it happened. For instance, many people get into uncomfortable corners because they fear to refuse the demands of hostile neurotics."

410. Fifty unhappy people came as a group to ask a teacher for helpful information. He told them, "The first information is that you really do not want my information, though you will insist that you do. If you can take this bit of information you may return tomorrow for more." The next day forty-nine were absent. The returning man glanced around the room and complimented the teacher, "You give accurate information."

411. In a class in Louisiana someone remarked, "Last week you said we must see all of another person, not

just a part. What does that mean?" Reply: "When seeing a domineering person, also see a desperately insecure person. But to do this you must not be frightened by his exterior pretense of strength."

412. Let cosmic science explain your emotions. Take dread. Cosmic science explains that dread is simply an incorrect movement of the emotional system. So study everything possible about this wrong movement. You will see that dread arises only when we promote or protect self-pleasing imaginations about ourselves. But we must also see imaginations *as* imaginations. Study all emotions this way, just as a geologist studies and explains volcanoes.

413. Said a teacher to his class, "Do not feel uncomfortable or annoyed when approached on the street by an unshaven human derelict. Just wait until you are able to recognize a shaven one."

414. The earth is surrounded by a protective barrier called the ozone layer. Located high in the sky, the ozone layer makes life on earth possible by shielding living things from harmful ultraviolet rays. We have a psychic ozone layer which protects us from all harm, including the harm we unknowingly bring upon ourselves. Your present reading will make this protective barrier stronger, also, you will understand perfectly how it operates in your day. For one thing, it protects you from harmful people.

415. The damage done by stubborn self-will can be illustrated. A discouraged pupil asked his piano teacher, "Why does my playing lack harmony?" The teacher sighed, "You have just one weakness. You insist upon playing *your* way instead of *the* way."

416. Like an actor who enjoys playing the role of a battling soldier, the world is in love with its destructive drama. However, any individual who ceases to love his dramatic conflicts and pains will soon see them vanish. Everything depends upon whether we choose the role or the real. Be wise. Choose the real.

417. The director of a museum was going through some dusty collections stored in a dark corner of the basement. One object wrapped in cheap cloth caught his eye. Removing the cloth he unrolled a rich Persian carpet once owned by a king. Though beautiful in color and design, the carpet had been forgotten for years. Man has forgotten himself, but can remember and unroll his royal nature. This leads to ease when with other people.

418. A good man observed that his neighbors carried burdensome sacks around. One carried a Sack of Gloom, another a Sack of Bitterness, and so on. Wishing to help them, the good man sought and found a high cliff from which the burdens could be dropped once and for all. But when telling everyone the good news he was astonished at how few people ever came to drop their burdens. He was informed by a wise man, "Most people cannot live without the odd thrill provided by their burdens. Freedom is above all such foolishness."

419. Asked a student in class, "Please discuss good feelings." Replied the teacher, "Authentic good feelings and feelings of vanity are often confused in people's minds. They fail to see that authentic good feelings are not the result of an action, such as public generosity, but are included in the very essence of private goodness." Ponder this profound principle.

420. Several hundred people heard a challenging truth-talk. Most of them went away while muttering,

"I don't see the necessity of him shaking me up like that." But a few thoughtful people departed while commenting, "I see the necessity of him shaking me up like that."

HOW AWARENESS BANISHES NERVOUSNESS

421. Awareness of the problem is half the solution. A Florida woman became aware of a particular nervousness in her day. She worried that things would go wrong with her social plans, as when having guests over for dinner. She then became aware of the mental and emotional slavery in worrying over the opinions of guests. Then, by no longer attributing power to the attitudes and judgments of others, she banished nervousness. Enrich yourself in this way.

422. Imagine someone dwelling in an unhealthy climate. Every day he struggles to cure himself of the aches and pains caused by the antagonistic weather, but fails. When advised by a doctor to move away from the disagreeable region he refuses to even listen. Is he valuable to himself or is he useless to himself? Useless. It is equally useless to try to cure a specific human ache as long as the sufferer insists upon remaining in his unhealthy mental climate. This book is your guide to a healthy inner climate.

423. A study group was discussing the absolute necessity of living from truthful principles. Someone commented, "But many people demand proof of the need for higher aims." Another member responded, "The perfect proof of the need for truth is the desperate lives of those who demand proof!"

424. A story written many years ago told of a city street where shops offered various services. There were a bakery, a jewelry shop, an inn. One shop offered a unique service, for after the owner's name was a description of his occupation: *Destroyer of Illusions*. Those who availed themselves of his unusual services returned home with new feelings toward life. So can you.

425. The world's foolishness is like a clever magician who plays a trick on you while diverting your attention with meaningless chatter. Never mind the kind of world society has created for itself. Do not carelessly accept it as yours. You have your own world to build. So regardless of what happens outside, continue to practice inside. You will then command the outside in a new way.

426. Migrating birds are credited with the discovery of dozens of islands in the Pacific Ocean, including Hawaii. Looking up at a flight of birds, the observers reasoned, "There must be a new land in that direction." That is what men and women need—the sensing of a new direction, inspired by an upward gaze.

427. Requested someone, "Please comment on our compulsive need to admire certain people." The comment was, "A person seeks in another what he feels is missing in himself. It is a common error among people, including students of truth. In fact, both admirer and admired wander in the same desert of delusion, each seeing the other according to neurotic needs."

428. You are trying to arrange a meeting with understanding. And understanding is also trying to arrange a meeting with you. Come to the right place yourself, and understanding will meet you there.

You will then blend with each other, like the tips of two searchlights meeting in a dark sky.

429. Existing on this planet are a few human beings who have achieved something seldom seen, which is kindness without a self-serving motive. Many people imagine they possess this virtue, but it is imagination only. The rare ones live the virtue without giving thought to it. Like the owner of a home, such a unique individual has the key he needs, which is knowledge of his cosmic nature.

430. The acclaimed Flemish painter, Peter Paul Rubens, once carried some of his paintings to Spain as a gift for royalty. A torrential rain penetrated the sealed boxes containing the paintings, damaging them. Someone suggested to Rubens that the pictures could be restored by another painter, but Rubens refused. Rubens said he would not mingle his own artistry with that of another painter. And so must every person be his own spiritual artist. If there is damage, only the artist himself can make it right.

431. Trying to find satisfaction in vanity-serving activities is as useless as reading the telephone book for entertainment. But they are never called vanity-serving activities. They are called contributions to social progress or additions to human understanding.

432. In a class in Michigan the teacher instructed the students to ask questions of each other. One student asked another, "How can we bring together the scattered pieces of our lives?" The reply was, "One method is to see the healthiness of the ideas we collect here. There is in fact freshness and health in this room, and one part of us feels it. A city-dweller has a similar feeling of natural health when viewing

a quiet country cornfield. Expand this impression of natural health."

433. The task of an awakened man is to show people that they do not know what they imagine they know. He asks them to stop talking as if they know what they are talking about. He points out, "A man who merely imagines he knows gold when seeing it can walk right past a mountain of gold without seeing it." The awakened man is not insulting the intelligence of people, but wishes to lead them to true intelligence in which there is no strife or envy or heartache.

434. Rain actually falls high above the desert, but fails to reach the ground below. This is because the water evaporates when striking a zone of hot and dry air. Man has his own zone of resistance and ignorance which prevents refreshing truth from reaching him. Receptivity changes everything, including your home life.

435. A teacher's assistant provided preliminary information to a new class. At one point he said, "There is one wrong attitude which will bar you from collecting what you need. It is an attitude of criticism toward the teacher. You may feel he is not considerate enough of your tender feelings, or that he fails to understand you. You may think you know more than he does, or that you already comprehend everything he says. Many who come here are unaware of this critical spirit. They leave as empty as they came."

436. Protecting stimulating but worthless ideas is as ridiculous as a soldier guarding a barrel of trash. One worthless notion hugged by self-deceiving man is that he can calm down his stormy life any morning he wishes. But of course that morning never comes.

437. A scientist invented a magic mirror which showed people as they were in fact, which meant it could reveal the flattering fantasies people had about themselves. Hearing about it a furious mob invaded and wrecked the scientist's laboratory. The mob's leader said to the dazed scientist, "Can't you see the consequences of denying people their self-images of being good and decent? Why, it might turn them toward violence."

438. Correction of what we are begins with seeing what we are. There is no other beginning. But what we are is so frightening to our vanities and images that we refuse to either look or admit. Denying our hidden negativities is as foolish as saying there are no rocks underground because we do not see them there. People insist they want to change. They can start by acting upon the fact in the first sentence of this paragraph.

439. Said a student to his teacher, "If I could predict human behavior I could save myself the grief of wrong involvements." Said the teacher, "You can always predict that a frightened horse will jump, though you cannot always predict its direction. But it is enough to be fully aware of its habit of jumping when feeling threatened. That will keep you at a safe distance."

440. What you *really* want for yourself is always trying to break through, just as a cooling breeze flows through an open window on a hot day. Your part is to open the windows of your mind.

THE ROAD TO COSMIC CONTENTMENT

441. A man can know the truth intellectually and still be separated from its rewards. Such a man cannot

understand why so much knowledge supplies so little contentment. Ask a prisoner whether he wishes to talk about the flowered fields he sees through his prison bars or whether he prefers to be in the fields. We must go beyond intellectualism to cosmic command.

442. Going around with wrong ideas is as awkward as wearing clothing several sizes too large. One such idea is to believe that one will be happy simply by obtaining whatever is desired. There is nothing like getting what you want to prove that you really did not want it! Has this ever happened to you?

443. One seeker began self-transformation by resolving to take his life back to himself. This resolution came after noticing how he had lost his own life to domineering people and to his own weaknesses. The very awareness of his unhappy condition aroused fresh energy for changing it. You can do the same. Resolve to recover your own life. It can be done.

444. "I will give you an especially profound fact to ponder," said a teacher to his class. "Suffering people secretly and wrongly believe there is a special virtue in their sorrow, which is why they refuse to give it up. No man ever ended suffering without first seeing its contribution to his flattering fantasies about himself. Your assignment is to ponder all this until tomorrow, when we will explore its deep meaning."

445. When British author John Milton finished a page of a manuscript he would immediately cut it to half the size. This gave his readers a clear and concise message having no useless words. We can give ourselves clear lives by cutting away useless traits, such as resistance to healing facts.

446. The teaching methods of one who really knows are unlike the procedures found in ordinary schools. This is because the teacher aims to create extraordinary men and women. In one class a new student frequently flashed mechanical smiles. He was instructed to not smile for the next two hours. He was both amused and educated by the attempt, for he saw for the first time how thoroughly he was controlled by mechanical forces.

447. After answering several questions from his audience, a real teacher said, "Now I will ask you a question. If everyone else in the world became the kind of person you are, what kind of world would it be?"

448. Remember the phrase *cosmic curiosity*. It teaches a right attitude toward the baffling and the troublesome. Have cosmic curiosity toward problems, instead of facing them with anxiety or with feelings of helplessness. This allows your natural powers to carry you to a higher place within yourself, a place of certain solutions. It is like climbing a tall tree in a thick jungle to gain a clear view of directions.

449. It is a great mistake to try to please people who demand to be pleased. Satisfy one demand and two more demands will arise. Neurotic needs are never satisfied. A demanding mind is like a hammer that sees everything as a nail. Remember that and stay out of the way. You owe nothing to demanding people.

450. Many years ago an Englishman left an oil lamp with a primitive African tribe. The tribesmen failed to use it for practical purposes. They worshipped the lamp for awhile, then destroyed it by poking at the glass with their spears. Because men and women make no persistent effort to understand cosmic light they deny themselves its guidance.

451. During the question and answer period after a lecture the speaker was asked, "Please make our problem clear to us." Response: "The problem is that what you know is all you know. Your present viewpoints make up your entire world. You cannot conceive anything outside of this familiar world and so make no effort to fly above it. Leave your world of limited thought to see life from the cosmic viewpoint, which is the total viewpoint."

452. When one is no longer prey to his own changing moods he is no longer bothered by the changing moods of other people. He is like a boat escaped to the open sea which no longer collides with the heavy traffic in the harbor. Having changed his psychological sea, he sails serenely. You can be free of everyone.

453. A man told his friend, "Today I stepped in front of a moving bus and didn't get hurt." The friend's eyes widened in wonderment as he gasped, "That was a miracle!" The other man said with a shrug, "Not really. The bus was moving backward." That story catches us by surprise because of the mind's habit of making automatic assumptions. By breaking the habit we also break the chain of automatic troubles caused by automatic assumptions.

454. A class member requested permission to make a comment. When the teacher nodded the student said, "One insight has helped me in a special way. I see the folly of trying to run away from ourselves with various distractions and excitements. It is as ridiculous as someone running into a closet to hide from himself. My awareness of the wrong way has opened the door to the new and right way." The right way is rich with power and pleasure.

455. Anyone can continue with his studies when feeling good. That will be rewarded all right, but it is nothing compared with the gold gained by working when discouraged. Working at self-knowledge when feeling low gives a healthy shock to our lazy parts, forcing them to get up and serve as they should. It is like a persistent African explorer who is suddenly joined and helped by natives he thought had deserted him.

456. A thoughtful review of all these facts will improve you every time, just as frequent rain makes the grass greener. For practice, go over the following fact several times: Rescue is never absent. We are.

457. In a class in New York City the topic of mind-conditioning arose. The teacher instructed with an illustration. "The mind," he explained, "is like a clean white cloth. If dipped into green dye the cloth becomes green; if immersed in blue dye it becomes blue. The dyes are the hundreds of acquired opinions and beliefs falsely cherished by man. For the mind to regain its original purity it must be dipped into Truth, which removes all conditioning."

458. Suppose a man showed you a single brick from his house. Would you buy his house with judgment based on that one brick? No. To have cosmic judgment, which alone is accurate, one must see the whole life-picture. Your reading aids in this.

459. Imagine a man tossing stones over a tall wall. The stones fall on the other side to injure people and destroy property. When told of the damage he is doing the man denies it, exclaiming indignantly, "I see no damage!" A blocking wall exists in man's mind, preventing him from seeing the damage he does to himself and others. This explains the curious condition

119

of someone who angrily denies that he is angry. Part of our healthy task is to break down this mental wall in order to see ourselves as we really are.

460. A girl complained to her mother that the hose in the back yard would not give water. The mother instructed, "See what is interfering." The girl discovered a twisted hose. What is interfering with our cosmic refreshment? A wish to lean on others? A lack of daring toward self-unification? Eliminate the interference. Your life will flow happily.

THE REAL MAGIC OF
AN AWAKENED MAN

461. An awakened man is a mental magician in the authentic meaning of that phrase. He could meet any stranger on the street and tell him a thousand facts about his psychic condition. For instance, he knows that when that stranger screams for something it is not the object that he values but the scream. But this magical insight has no value to the unawakened man because of his inability and his refusal to listen to it. He is like a man who refuses to move out of a building condemned by the city inspector because he *calls* it his castle.

462. "Something said in class last week was of great benefit," remarked a student. "You said we must have no hesitation in disappointing people who wish to dominate us, but must do it with the motive of setting ourselves free, not to hurt the domineering person. I now see how I feared to disappoint people. That slavery will end. Thank you." His victory can be your victory.

463. Whatever is impossible on the level of ordinary thought becomes possible on the higher level of cosmic insight. Take someone who promises to not

get angry or to not speak harshly. His promise will vanish like a bird into the bush, for usual thought is powerless to obey itself. However, his very insight into the incompetence of ordinary thought becomes his first upward step toward cosmic insight. Now he is gaining power for extraordinary self-transformation.

464. Scientists are researching the possibility of harnessing the power of electricity residing in storms. The tremendous energy now unused could light up cities and move machinery. Likewise, any individual can learn how to use the power found in psychic storms for enlightened living. The energy alive in grief or frustration can move anyone toward a new world.

465. Plato was so eager for cosmic knowledge that he once paid the equivalent of twelve hundred dollars for just three books. Those who gain higher wisdom are those who place a high value on it. Think often about this. It leads to skill in handling people.

466. A student in Wisconsin told the rest of the class, "I will tell you of a stage I had to pass through. I had to see the emptiness of most advice about self-rescue. I am not criticizing anyone. I simply saw that the advisor and the advised were equally pathetic, like two sinking ships looking to each other for rescue. My mind is now clear on this. Only that rare person who has first rescued himself can throw a rope to others."

467. Some people think they can bargain with the truth as if it were a commercial product. Having nothing of real value to give, their attempts will fail. They are vainly trying to buy the products of a prosperous nation with the worthless currency of a bankrupt country. They *could* come with what they actually have—their poverty—for Truth welcomes such honesty.

468. No one should complain, "Why was I deceived by that person?" He must ask instead, "What in me was on the same level as that deception?" That is the only way to remain undeceived. An eagle on a mountain is not captured by a wolf in the valley.

469. Whoever takes command of these principles will find himself taking command of daily life in a new and exciting way. For example, he is able to think more logically and profitably in the area of time. He accomplishes more in less time, and this without nervous haste. He does the more important tasks first, he allows time for the unexpected. Such a man is like a competent manager of a factory whose knowledge of the parts of a product gives him command of the whole operation.

470. People are like books with the wrong jackets; they are not what they seem. A good loser is simply someone who is a skilled actor. And when someone tells you his conscience prevents him from doing a certain thing he really means he sees nothing in it for himself. See people as they are, not as they appear to be.

471. "In what way," asked a student, "do I separate myself from my real nature?" Answer: "You fear the angry and neurotic outbursts of people. In an attempt to keep them pleased you say and do things which are false to your real nature, which is self-division. See this in your social contacts. Illuminate your mind, then such fears will no longer be part of you."

472. The opportunity to learn in a class must be preceded by something real within the individual which wishes to take the opportunity. Where there is a carrot but no rabbit, or a rabbit but no carrot, nothing happens. But watch what happens when carrot and rabbit meet.

473. At the start of the inner journey we have so many conflicting maps we switch this way and that in self-doubt. Then by sensing the errors in all but one map, an audacious confidence arises. We must still study the right map and must go on with the journey, but it is now the only real pleasure in life.

474. Examine the elation of gaining more money or making a sexual conquest or winning public honor. This elation is a subtle form of suffering, though rarely seen as this by the distracted sufferer. Such elation contains its opposite. Sooner or later it must plunge down from the heights to depression and anxiety. It is the elation of a conquering tyrant who must now live in fear of being conquered by other tyrants. Understanding alone supplies liberation from the tyranny of false elation.

475. Some Canadian zoologists set out to photograph some of the rarer animals of an unfamiliar region. Proceeding toward the area, they picked up different supplies at different stops along the way. When all necessary equipment was obtained they penetrated the region with excellent results. Similarly, you are now equipping yourself with new thoughts, with life-changing insights, with unique plans. Excellent results are just ahead.

476. A lawyer attended a study group for the first time. During the open discussion he admitted, "I fear that these teachings may ask me to give up things I want to keep." He was told, "The only things you are asked to give up are those things which do absolutely nothing for your real life." The lawyer nodded in understanding.

477. You will understand human error better by seeing one of them quite clearly. No person is *really* interested in a political or religious or social cause. Lonely and

afraid, a man uses a cause as a lifeboat by which he hopes to navigate to a more secure world. In spite of exterior pretenses of enthusiasm, he senses he cannot reach the other shore, for another part of him knows that only the Inner Voyage can take him there.

478. Remember that what you call success or failure are simply human points of view. There exists definitely a Supreme point of view which is above these opposites, just as the sun exists above land and sea. Seek within for this liberating Supreme Viewpoint. You will then have power and pleasure in human relations.

479. A businessman was pressured into accepting a role in a play presented by a community drama group. Later, when regretting his weakness in accepting, he politely dropped out. Do not let others cast you in the role they want you to play for their personal benefit. Many who play the roles of protective friends or helpful neighbors wish they had not accepted the script handed them. Be aware of this subtle trick and refuse it. Your life is yours.

480. Two orators of ancient Rome were called upon for speeches. One talked eloquently for a full hour. The other then arose to announce, "Men of Rome, everything that he has said, I will do." Do what you know.

THE SEARCH IN A HAUNTED HOUSE

481. A novel of the last century tells about an ill man who is told where to find the rare medicine he needs. It is hidden somewhere in a haunted mansion. The man is compelled to search the haunted house, room by room, facing new terrors in each. But he finds the medicine and cures himself. Life-cure is certain for whoever will search through his inner rooms.

482. A student asked a teacher, "Why can't I make myself persist toward a desired goal?" The teacher answered, "Because you wrongly assume that the self which decides upon the goal will be the same self in command a week later. It will not be in control because man is split into dozens of shifting and contradictory selves. Your goal is at their mercy, like a ball kicked in every direction by racing children. This is why you must seek self-unity."

483. Diligence in the acquisition of self-understanding is a simple but noble virtue. The future is always bright for the diligent seeker, for just as every dictionary explains the nature of a dictionary, every man can explain himself to himself.

484. Do not let strong feelings convince you that you are right about something. We often feel right but later pay the price because we were actually wrong. We are so in love with strong emotions that we permit them to deceive us, like a foolish man who permits himself to be carried away by the fiery oratory of a dictator. Strong feelings deceive us when we vigorously defend false ideas. We may win a thrill from it but we lose ourselves.

485. Looking down upon earth, two angels agreed upon a research program. One was to count all the truly self-enlightened human beings on earth, while the other was to number the self-deluded. The angel counting the wise individuals was through within a few minutes. The other angel is still counting.

486. Satisfy yourself as to the rightness of these procedures. It can be done. However, a preliminary stage is necessary. It consists of a deep and lasting conviction that the old ways can take you nowhere. Insight into uselessness reveals the useful. It is like a small child who

finally realizes he cannot force a left shoe onto a right foot, which reveals the right way. Go through the preliminary stage and satisfaction is certain.

487. During a group's open discussion, a student said, "When first meeting these ideas I felt hesitant toward them. I was like a timid diver about to plunge down from a new height. The timidity passed, to be replaced by a feeling of wonder. I mean it was a wonder to realize that *something else* did exist after all."

488. If you wish to discover the secret facts about a person or an event, get yourself out of the way. Discovery occurs in the absence of the habitual self. Then, there is not a self which understands, but a blending of self and understanding into one unit, just as a rainbow and its beauty are one.

489. Anyone having the hobby of carving objects out of wood must know the characteristics of various woods. He must know that pine is soft, that hickory is hard and that cherry has rich colors. Knowledge of human characteristics is equally necessary if we are to carve new lives for ourselves. Knowledge heals human relations.

490. An expert demon was instructing a class of student demons. He stated, "Remember that people really do not want happiness, rather, they crave thrills. You see, their deluded minds mistake thrills for happiness. Take anger. When you provoke a man into anger he has a sick love for the thrill of his self-destructive anger. He actually takes it as a type of happiness! Man is incredibly ill, and his denial of the illness plays right into your hands. Believe me, gentlemen, man's stupidity makes your task much easier than you can imagine."

491. Think beyond yourself. Feel beyond yourself. Walk beyond yourself. Why? Because this is what a certain part of you wants more than anything else. Make it the supreme part. Then, like a fugitive who has reached the border of a friendly country, you will no longer need to run through life.

492. When a difficulty is truly understood it ceases to be a difficulty. The mind itself is the difficulty, so the only right action is to change the mind. But since most people are reluctant to do this, the sure solution eludes them. Do not be like most people. Someday you will zoom upward to the new view, just as an underwater swimmer breaks through the surface of the sea.

493. Said a teacher to some new students, "If we stumble around the darkness in earnest search of a lamp, we will not remain in darkness. We succeed by realizing how stumbling our steps really are, by not pretending that the stumbling is a waltz."

494. A pack of wolves declared war on some neighboring animals. But feeling guilty over starting the war the wolves asked a counselor for a way to hide from their guilt. The counselor smiled confidently and said, "The coffee-and-doughnuts method has worked superbly for centuries. It goes like this. Every time you hurt an enemy immediately give him coffee and doughnuts. For awhile this will make you feel wonderfully compassionate, during which time you can practice endless cruelties without feeling guilty."

495. French artist Claude Vernet was on board a ship caught in a raging tempest. The ship's captain was amazed to see Vernet bracing himself on deck while eagerly sketching the mountainous waves. The cosmic artist is equally observant. Instead of cringing before

inner storms, he studies them. His new knowledge then becomes a power for calming the psychic waves.

496. A boy and his parents took frequent trips to a distant city. The highway led through dozens of small towns. On one trip the parents were astonished to learn that their son knew the name of every village. He explained casually, "I like to know where I am." Gain knowledge of your inner location.

497. A duke was imprisoned in a tower by an outlaw chief. The single window provided a view of an empty field below. After two months the duke saw a wandering minstrel singing in the field, so the nobleman quickly wrote out and tossed down a note appealing for help. The note went to the king who soon rescued the duke. Only later did the duke realize that with more attentiveness he could have been rescued much sooner, for the minstrel had come to the field every day to sing. Increase your attentiveness to rescuing lessons.

498. Add the following to your knowledge. Only a person with a conscious point in him can learn from a conscious man. Anyone living solely from unconscious parts can hear cosmic counsel but will deceive himself into believing he understands and lives it. This explains why an unconscious man persists with his mechanical habit of hurting other people. He is like a ghost who must find a house to haunt.

499. A baffled student asked in class, "Can't we learn about ourselves just through daily experiences? Why all this emphasis on self-study?" He heard, "Can you learn the valuable contents of a book just by carrying it around—or must you open it?"

500. Men dwell in delusion about their condition, but only someone outside of delusion knows about it.

A man found himself inside a huge building where people lived in both towers and dungeons. The tower-people told him, "We love living in the towers of this castle." The dungeon-dwellers told him, "We live down here in the castle but hope to make it up to the towers." Stepping outside the man peered closely at the building—and froze in horror. What both groups had called a castle was in fact a heavily barred prison.

HOW TO USE COSMIC AID PROFITABLY

501. A speaker gave several solutions to the human predicament. One hearer thought as he left the hall, "I wish the seats had been more comfortable." A second hearer thought, "Shall I have a salad or a sandwich for lunch?" A third hearer thought, "Maybe I have time to catch that television program." But none thought, "How can I use that message to turn my life upward?"

502. Disappointment with yourself is like coming to a fork in the road. One can turn in the right or the wrong direction. To choose rightly, do not be disappointed over failure to become financially successful or failure to find romance with the opposite sex. Instead, see disappointment as a call to inner correction. Inward success ends all disappointment. Self-wholeness is self-contentment.

503. What is called social progress is merely a new arrangement of an old disaster. It is a second hurricane which scatters everyone toward a different cave. Make inner progress by peering closely at this fact until seeing it deeply.

504. The rescuing facts are utterly simple, as simple as breathing. For instance, whoever deceives himself

about his true nature and its actual relationship with Reality will deceive himself about everything else—and pay the price. But whoever knows his real nature is rewarded by his very cosmic knowledge. What is simpler than that?

505. Man's ridiculous behavior is caused by ignorance of natural laws of how life really works. A foolish man rode his horse onto a ship about to cross a stretch of sea. When asked why he rode the horse around the deck he replied, "Because I want to get there faster."

506. To realize something one never realized before —that is what the spiritual adventure is all about. Realization is the same as self-release, as the ending of illusion, the same as finding a totally new path. A building contractor in Chicago arrived at a magnificent realization. He realized that there is only one right rebellion on earth—rebellion against his own self-defeating unawareness.

507. A group of lost hikers argued among themselves as to which of several paths led out of the wilderness. One hiker definitely sensed the right path, but the others ignored his reasonings. He saw the necessity of parting company with the others, which he did, which brought him out of the wilderness. Self-rescue requires self-independence. The truly brave stand alone.

508. If you tell a wounded soldier that his injuries resulted from his engagement in a battle, he will believe you. But the most difficult task on earth is to convince a suffering citizen that he is an active contributor to the very society which injures him. Only deep insight into himself can heal him. You can win this insight.

509. A woman told the rest of the class, "For a long time I lived compulsively. I was like a woman doing a frenzied dance she did not know how to stop. Then I saw something. I saw the connection between my own wrong thoughts and the wrong things that happened to me. So I am changing my thinking. Maybe this revelation will help you as much as it helped me."

510. Constantly seek and remove obstacles to mental rebirth. With one person it might be a stubborn clinging to the very ways which injure him. To a second man it might be insufficient information about his emotions. A third person could be losing himself in pursuit of weird and useless systems. A fourth man might be unaware of how imagination weakens reason. Remove your own obstacles, which clarifies everything, just as music becomes clearer as you open the doors between you and the orchestra.

511. I will remind you of something about human ways. Many people will try to get you to think for them, will subtly try to burden you with mental work belonging to them alone. Be aware of this and politely refuse the burden, feeling no guilt over it. Do not carry a man across your bridge, however, you may wish to show him how to build his own bridge.

512. A fox or a hawk cannot escape the results of being a fox or a hawk. No man can escape the results of being the kind of person he is. Anger is its own punishment. Envy is its own burden. Deceit is its own pain. Remember this simple and this superb lesson.

513. Asked a teacher of his students, "Does a man in his right senses do anything to harm himself? Does a sensible man act in a way which results in anxiety and depression? Now what if you honestly find you are

not thinking and acting sensibly, that you are inviting grief? Does that not arouse energy for changing from self-defeating to self-rewarding action? Certainly it does."

514. A man dreamed of becoming the powerful ruler of the land. By schemes and by battles he achieved his goal. But shortly after taking power he felt strangely depressed and irritated. He consulted a wise man who told him, "While battling for power you thought you knew who you were, for instance, you called yourself the leader of a great social crusade. But by winning your goal you lost your self-advertising. You are now depressed because you no longer know who you are. Are you interested in knowing who you really are?"

515. Expectations, while appearing pleasant, ruin one's opportunity to live fully each day. Expectations arise from one's anxious need to find something in the future, such as security or excitement. But such expectations are under the illusion that man lives in time. A person owning an orchard today has no need to hope for fruit tomorrow. You own the orchard today.

516. If wishing to compose music you proceed with certain basic rules. You learn the principles of harmony, you select the notes you want, and so on. There is one thing you do not do. You do not copy another musician's composition. Creating life-harmony proceeds in a similar manner. Following right rules, you create your own composition, which alone is satisfying.

517. Trapped in a net of his own illusions, man tries to cut his way out with a knife—also illusory. Ask anyone, "What is real to you?" and his honest answer would be, "My pain and my puzzlement." Does anyone need any other reason for starting to walk in a different direction? Ahead of you is a marvelous journey.

518. A student gave a short talk before his group. At one point he said, "If what you do for yourself does nothing, why continue in that wrong way? Why continue to paddle a boat with a tennis racket? Our old natures are reluctant to give up wrong ways, so we must work against the old and the habitual. The new way can be found in this class. Look for it. Real progress reveals itself in less gloom each day, less boredom, less loneliness."

519. Men and women look at their frantic chase through life and wonder what Truth can do about it. If you ask the same question, reply, "What can the sun do to darkness?"

520. A frightened man habitually fawned slavishly before people he believed were wiser or stronger than he was. In order to please their minds he abandoned his own mind. But getting tired of his weakness he decided to fawn no more. To his delight and astonishment he discovered that this act ended his fear. Also, interestingly, he no longer saw the others as wise or strong. He saw them as foolish and weak. You can have the same enlightening experience.

THE PRACTICAL POWER OF TRUTH

521. A teacher's talk included, "Never forget that falseness can be very attractive and charming, like a pit covered with colorful flowers. In their misunderstanding, people mistake attractiveness for rightness, only to wake up too late. Wake up now and prevent a fall. See how practical this is?"

522. A boy living in a peaceful land was captured by a band of ruthless outlaws who masqueraded as

innocent travelers. The band's propaganda convinced the boy he was one of them. Over the years he was taught how to wear the right disguises in order to deceive and defeat enemies. But one day, when strongly feeling the unnaturalness of his disguises, he left the outlaws to return to his peaceful home. A person begins earnest work on himself when first sensing he is not who he imagines he is. The end of the masquerade is the start of peace.

523. When next meeting someone who tries to impress you in some way, use it as a lesson. Do this by seeing the person as someone chained by insecurity and tension. This helps deepen the understanding that one suffers only from oneself. One student found this lesson so interesting he gave the class a ten minute talk on it.

524. An orchardist in Iran captured a wild horse which was forced to work in the fields. But the horse rebelled so persistently against its unnatural servitude that the orchardist set him free. The man was pleased at his own feeling of relief and freedom. By psychic law, each time we set another person free from our demands we free ourselves of the anxiety which always exists in demands.

525. Men and women perpetuate their grief by falsely valuing it. A woman lost her pet parrot when it flew away. A week later she lost a ring. A friend asked her whether she was grieving over the loss of the ring. She replied, "No, there's still lots of grief left with that parrot." Do not glorify grief.

526. A scientist at a large university had an urgent need for detailed information about a rare plant growing in Honduras. He spent weeks making contacts

in Honduras, but the received information was scanty. Then, with both embarrassment and pleasure, he found the needed information in a book in his home library. The information needed for self-transformation is as close as our own minds. And self-change will change and enrich your human relations.

527. A spiritual teacher and his followers were walking down a road. The teacher wished to impress upon his disciples the need for complete devotion to truth. "Compromise," he declared, "can only thwart your wish for self-liberty." When reaching a fork in the road he illustrated his lesson by saying, "Before you are two roads. Walk down both of them at the same time."

528. When you do not think about who you are you do not know who you are. It is wrong thinking that attaches the labels of "success" or "failure" or "loved" or "rejected." Now, it is not frightening to not know who you are, to the contrary, it is the surprising secret of authentic happiness. Absence of self-labels is absence of anxiety. Once seeing this you can think rightly toward everyday affairs, while handling everything else with cosmic consciousness. You now live like a man on a mountaintop who has a beautiful view whichever way he turns.

529. In days when pirates roamed the seas a studious merchant was shipping his private library from England to his new home in India. The ship was halted by gold-hungry pirates, but seeing only a cargo of books, the pirates let the floating library resume its peaceful voyage. It is a curious fact that practical society has little interest in anyone who possesses true values.

530. A teacher told his students they would be given two sentences to think about for the next twenty-four

hours. He then said, "Instead of trying to change yourself, why not let yourself change? Now you have it!"

531. People worry, "But how can a weak and uncertain person like me do what must be done?" There is no reason for worry. You can do what must be done. Your own yearning nature is the only power needed, and it is always available, for it is never outside you. Just as an underground seed has within itself a spontaneous wish to grow upward into air and sunlight, so does your real nature wish to emerge into cosmic sunlight. Let it grow as it wishes.

532. A teacher's lesson began, "You are trying to tell the color of a cat by using the sense of feeling instead of the sense of sight. I mean that you are using a wrong spiritual method. You are trying to use ordinary thinking to obtain extraordinary facts, which cannot be done. Today you will develop a higher sense of perception. Start by having a receptive mind."

533. The startling has power for awakening. One inquirer discovered this for himself when first attending an esoteric study group. He told the class about certain doctrines and creeds he had been taught since boyhood. He felt how wrong and useless they were, yet felt uncomfortable about abandoning them. One startling question from a group member set him on the right road at last. The question was, "Why should you be loyal to what is damaging you?"

534. When you enter a relationship with another person, only two important factors are involved—the kind of person he is and the kind of person you are. The appearance of the house is nothing; the nature of the dweller is everything. Never forget this.

535. A pair of demons were in the business of selling evil schemes. But business was dull one day, causing one of the demons to complain anxiously, "I hope people are not improving." The other demon replied, "Cheer up. You just don't have enough faith in human nature." Sure enough, business was much better the next day.

536. Understand that you are embarking upon a different kind of self-action. You are not trying to improve your surface personality, not trying to appear more attractive or wise in public. *You are trying to change who you are.* See these two ideas—surface change and internal change of who you are. These two ideas are as far apart as sea from star. Remind yourself of this often, remembering who you are trying to change.

537. "I will give you a simple but profound method for seeing what another person is really like," a teacher informed his class. "When someone seizes upon the slightest opportunity to tell you the kind of person he is, he is telling you the kind of person he is not." This method ends gullibility.

538. In ancient Greece there lived a merchant with a deep yearning to find the answers to life. His spiritual hunger was satisfied by regular visits to a library containing scrolls which revealed secret wisdoms. When a furious storm struck the village, everyone scrambled to save personal property—everyone but the merchant. At considerable personal expense he hired workmen to protect and save the library. His action revealed what he valued above all else. Value life-enriching facts above all else.

539. Centuries ago in Sweden some imposters represented themselves as ambassadors from foreign

nations. To test those claiming to be ambassadors, the Swedish king asked them certain questions which only real ambassadors could answer correctly. The real parts within each person know the answers to life.

540. Imagine yourself talking with three captives in a camp for prisoners of war. You ask each about his chief aim in life. One says he wants to become a champion athlete, another states his wish to be elected mayor, while the third says he wants to become a wealthy man. You sadly realize what has happened. Captivity has so dulled their minds that they no longer see that their first aim must be to escape the camp. The same has happened to man. Captured by exterior glitter, he has forgotten his need to return home to himself.

INNER ILLUMINATION IS EVERYTHING

541. A real teacher entered the lecture hall and looked over his audience. He knew the hidden thoughts and attitudes of those before him. He began his talk by saying, "Some of you will succeed. You will succeed because you came here not to obtain a sense of security but to obtain inner illumination which is free from a tense demand for security."

542. No man meets harm unless he has first deceived himself about something. So cosmic honesty is perfect self-protection. But to convince someone of this is like trying to teach a sheep to value gold. End self-deception and you end problems with people.

543. A man living from an unconscious self-picture of being an intellectual tried to impress a teacher and

his students. The man claimed, "I see many things which you do not see." After boasting about himself for several minutes the man departed, gullibly believing he had made a favorable impression on everyone. The students asked their teacher, "Is it possible he sees many things?" The teacher explained, "Yes, but so does a man standing on his head."

544. The mere possession of spiritual or psychological facts means nothing unless the possessor also has a deep and sincere wish for self-transformation. Having facts without a wish to become a new person is like having a phone book but no phone.

545. When anyone is wasting his life there is no direct way to inform him of it. Incapable of cosmic hearing, he would scorn and spurn the idea that he is wasting himself. He is still a child trying to capture soap bubbles, giving the bubbles names such as *success* and *respectability.* Can nothing be done for him? Only he can do something for himself. It can start with an accepted jolt—the jolt of seeing the concealed terror in playing childish games.

546. A scientist lived in a remote cabin in the wilderness. One night he heard a radio lecture containing some information he needed badly. But the broadcast had come from far away, and was faint and unclear. For several weeks the scientist stayed close to his radio, hoping to hear the message again. He was rewarded when the lecture was repeated. Once you hear Truth's first faint message, come close and stay close.

547. Said a teacher, "Seeing something and understanding what you see are two different things. Do you understand the nature of a home by seeing its exterior? No. You must observe the nature of those who dwell

inside. The seeing of life changes into an understanding of life as you observe human nature as it is in fact, which may be quite different from what it appears to be."

548. Imagine someone offered either the original *Mona Lisa* or a substitute — and he chooses the substitute. Man chooses substitute religion, substitute intelligence, substitute action, then wonders why his busy life feels so worthless. Aim for the worthy.

549. Perhaps the idea of working within yourself to change your life is new and unfamiliar. Never mind how different it may appear just now. Just start in any way you like, for example, notice how certain words from you cause another person to respond in a certain way. Remember that inner rightness eventually expresses itself in outer rightness, just as certain weather conditions produce a rainbow.

550. At the end of a class a leader of an esoteric school gave his students a parting encouragement. "If you ever feel incapable of grasping these facts," he said, "you need do just one thing — go ahead anyway. That is all you need to do — just go ahead anyway."

551. Many people who say they want to be serious about their lives here on earth are deceiving themselves. They think they are serious when they are merely glum or puzzled over a problem. Sooner or later they depart from a study group, lacking consciousness of the diamonds they held in their hands so briefly. Worthwhile seriousness comes to those who abandon the thought, "I already know what is best." Self-honesty always attracts a reward.

552. Imagine several packages of vegetable seeds which were packed carelessly, so that a gardener expecting carrots comes up with lettuce. Man receives the unexpected and unwanted because he carelessly accepts labels in place of realities.

553. A class was guided by hearing, "People try to satisfy themselves with a daily diet of thrills and surprises and new experiences. But they are never satisfied, never, though they may outwardly appear contented. You might as well try to satisfy a horse's hunger by entertaining him with television. The false needs of false personality cannot be satisfied by anything. The only solution is to replace surface personality with essence."

554. A wolf told his cubs, "I myself have failed to lead a kindly life, so I want you to do better. I want each of you to be known as a kindly wolf." The cubs agreed. So from that day forward they never attacked sheep without wearing a collar on which was printed *Kindly Wolf.* The lesson? Do not believe in shallow human labels.

555. A doctor in Panama was treating some patients in an isolated village. Needing a certain medicine, he sent a message back to a hospital many miles away. The hospital replied that the medicine was not available. The doctor directed. "Look in the right place." When the doctor's precise instructions were followed, the medicine was promptly located. You, the reader, are now looking in the right place for the kind of medicine you may need.

556. A child peers into the dark back yard and is fearful. Why? A child is afraid of the dark only when he fails to understand the nature of the dark. The dark

is not a threat, as his fearful imagination supposes, but merely a natural condition. Any fearful threat in life turns into a harmless condition the moment our own consciousness shines upon it. What happens to the child's fear when his father turns on the back yard lights?

557. A teacher held a clean and attractive stone up before the class. He explained, "I picked this up just after it fell from the bank to splash into the stream." He then went on to explain that a fall from our present position is necessary if we are ever to be cleansed in the stream of Reality.

558. Two friends were having a conversation when one of them did a peculiar thing. He placed a banana on his head and marched backward around the room. He explained, "I have been troubled lately, so I went to a famous advisor who told me to do this." The friend asked, "But did he tell you what good it would do?" The troubled man scoffed, "Don't be silly. When you pay hard-earned money for advice you don't question it."

559. There is a sure method for discovering what a man or woman is really like. Just observe his reaction when told unpleasant truths about himself. This tests his readiness for rescue. A painful reaction is certain, however, can he use it wisely? Can he go on from there to see that the pain is caused by nothing more than psychic heedlessness? If so, he is ready, like a weary wanderer who no longer minds the stormy road, for he knows it leads home.

560. Why wonder what is on the other side of the mountain when you can see for yourself? Of course, there is the small matter of making the climb. Since there is a way to climb over the top, there is no reason to hesitate. If you have been applying these ideas as best you can, you are already on higher ground.

HOW TO KNOW WHO YOU ARE

561. You do not try to hear an apple. Neither do you try to see a sound. Wrong powers cannot produce right results. It is equally useless to try to use only memory for living a whole life. Go beyond memory. Start by pondering the meaning of going beyond your storehouse of acquired information. Do you know who you really are? You will know when going beyond all memories of who you are. To find yourself, lose yourself. Does that sound familiar?

562. Captain James Cook, the English navigator and explorer, carried with him on his voyages a variety of seeds and flowers found in the countryside of England. He planted a few seeds wherever he landed. In time, a part of England flowered in hundreds of lands throughout the world. The illuminated individual performs a similar service. His seeds of wisdom are released wherever he goes, needing only receptive ground in order to flourish. With these teachings you can grow a new life.

563. A class in Oregon was invited to relate personal experiences. A salesman said, "Until coming to this group I was like someone trying to walk a straight line in a field of boulders. Thanks to the help received here I am eliminating the boulders. For example, there is much less tendency to feel indignant when denied something."

564. Man is battered by unconscious forces, like a ship pounded at night by titanic waves. The seas are calmed by self-knowledge. If elation over a success is followed by depression, it was a success in the eyes of society and yourself, but not in the eyes of Reality. If feeling confident after a compliment it was a

temporary stimulation, which is quite different from the steady confidence of one's real nature.

565. A stove is influenced by its own heat. A man is influenced by his own nature. It appears that harmful influences come from the words and actions of others, but it is only an appearance. A man is influenced only by being the kind of a person he is. Know that your real nature can encounter an event without being harmfully influenced by it. Your real nature is all-powerful.

566. When reading phrases such as "higher world" and "another shore" you should take them as simple aids to understanding. This "higher world" does not exist in time and space and is therefore not apart from you, though it may be unseen as yet. The "higher world" appears in the here and now to a conscious person, but not to those who dwell only on the mental plane. One understanding student explained, "To find the higher world is to find yourself, for they are in fact One World."

567. Truth is like a river flowing gently through a dark and treacherous jungle. The wise and safe man remains in his boat and follows the winding course of the river. The unwise and apprehensive man tries to hack his own shortcut through the jungle.

568. Someone asked, "How can society cure its confusion?" Reply: "It can't. Take any organization discussing a fiery issue of the day. Included in that group will be at least one man whose only contribution will be that of confusion. He really has nothing to say but loves to hear himself saying it. Now, will you ask *him* to end the confusion in that room? That man represents society as a whole, which is the cause of confusion, not the cure. Mental clarity and cosmic consciousness are the same."

569. A small boy remarked that he disliked squash but had forgotten why. Man has the same lapse of memory. He has forgotten why chaos continues—because he accepts everything but cosmic facts. He has forgotten why he must change—because contentment is better than agony. With the aid of cosmic science he can remember what must be remembered. It can be done. I can tell you it can be done.

570. Some seekers approached a mystic master to request, "Please show us how to stop living useless and miserable lives." The teacher began by revealing unpleasant facts about each seeker. He was soon interrupted by indignant cries of, "Wait! Why are you trying to destroy our good and noble lives?"

571. Centuries ago there lived a kindly king whose palace was on a mountaintop. Hearing that some of his subjects in the valleys below lacked food, he directed that fine and rare fruits should be gathered from the royal orchards. The fruit was placed in a gentle stream where it was carried down to the hungry people. But only those who had visited the king's domain could recognize the unique fruit as the food they needed. Their hunger was satisfied. In life, we must make ourselves ready to recognize and receive the satisfying Truth.

572. A teacher informed a class in human relations, "The way you offend another person is the same way you fear being offended by the other. Wrath fears wrath. Irresponsibility dreads irresponsibility. Therefore, a whole person fears no one."

573. Remember the difference between your mechanical energy and conscious energy. Mechanical energy serves the activities of daily life, but it cannot show you who you really are. Conscious energy alone has power

145

to make you different, to carry you to a new place. Mechanical energy can bring you to the edge of the woods, but only conscious energy can reveal the astounding secrets within the woods. Do you know what you must do when reaching the entrance to the woods? Bravely enter. You will safely exit.

574. There is a humorous story about a man sitting glumly in his boat which is tied to the dock. Someone asks him why he does not sail the sea. He replies, "See that other boat out there? Well, there may be wind enough just for it." Man limits his mind and then glumly complains of a limited life.

575. "What was meant," a student asked a teacher, "when you said that pain is caused by unconsciousness?" The teacher explained, "Take any small pain, like the faint feeling of depression felt when the first few people at a party say good night and leave. You are pained because the happy party is ending. Now, you felt the pain but you were not conscious of it, just as you feel a cup but never think about it. You end painful feelings when consciousness takes command. We will discuss this again."

576. Several companies dealing in flavors and spices heard about an unusual kind of a vanilla plant growing in a tropical forest. Only one company investigated what they heard, and that one company emerged from the forest with a superior kind of vanilla. One word should be sufficient for those wishing a life of unusual flavor: Investigate!

577. A class was discussing the problems and the pains of being a self-divided person. One student volunteered to define self-division: "A self-divided man is

one who praises himself for his successes but blames others for his failures."

578. A businessman was asked why he had ceased to handle an inexpensive but inferior brand of paint. He answered, "Because I now recognize a wrong move as being wrong." That is what we seek—an instant talent for recognizing a wrong move. Recognition is our very power of deliverance! Anyone seeing the folly of trying to buy friendship will no longer suffer the strain of that wrong move.

579. Because of nervous doubts, people change their minds as fast as a hummingbird changes directions. Living with painful doubts indicates that one still dwells on the mental plane. Those living on the cosmic level have no doubts about themselves or anything else. They *know*. Join them.

580. A truly independent thinker is one who has freed himself from compulsive thinking. One such thinker was challenged by some well-dressed men who considered themselves intellectuals. When the thinker had a chance to speak he said to them, "You defend your present ways of thinking. Really now, in your private lives is it fortunate or unfortunate to be under their domination?"

TAKE THE LEAP TOWARD SELF-NEWNESS

581. Make a conscious aim to realize the existence of a totally unique way to live on earth, a way without personal conflict. This uniqueness is attained by those who do their part, by those who are willing to take the leap. The thoughts and programs in this book will

assist your aim. Use them daily. Knowledge is a ladder, so be an eager climber.

582. A class heard, "A small child is absorbed with toys because all he knows is his toys. Try to interest the child in something more meaningful than toys, perhaps a book or a tool and he will stare blankly at them. But a growing child grows tired of toys. How many human beings outgrow social toys?"

583. Imagine a flock of scared sparrows caught in a storm who turn to each other for guidance. So do desperate men turn to other desperate men for help. What can be done about personal desperation? Do not feel ashamed of it. Do not enjoy its strange stimulation. Rely on no exterior source of relief. Realize that self-knowledge can end it.

584. As their airplane took off, two businessmen began a casual conversation. One asked the other, "What is the purpose of your trip?" The other man said, "I'm returning to our home office to straighten it out." A person's purpose in the business of life should be to straighten out the home office—himself.

585. Millions of men and women believe they can win an argument with Truth. It is a sad illusion, causing defeat and despair. One can argue with friends and relatives, but not with Truth. Do you see why? Truth never argues. Would the sun argue with a candle regarding the power of light? Never. Those who assume they are arguing with Truth are really arguing with something wrong within themselves. The agonizing argument ends when one sees that Truth wishes to deprive him of just one thing—his hidden tragedy.

586. Said a new member of a class to the teacher, "I have a comment about something discussed last night. You said we must have something real in us before we can distinguish between a real and an artificial teaching. I don't understand." The teacher replied, "Can an artificial bird recognize a real bird? It is like that."

587. Frustration. That is the haunting horror. Frustration turned in the right direction. That is the great action available to all. The right direction is an inward turn which reveals why one thinks and acts the way he does. Remember, the inflow of fresh self-insight can dissolve frustrations of every shape, just as an ocean wave smooths out the entire stretch of sand.

588. A teacher of commercial subjects was instructing his class of adults on the topic of business efficiency. As a practical experiment he instructed everyone to find a shorter route when driving from home to class. Fourteen out of twenty students were able to do so. It is a pleasantly practical experiment when anyone examines his daily ways to become more efficient. Efficiency is an outcome of self-knowledge.

589. A student of Truth invited a friend to accompany him to a lecture. As they waited for the talk to begin the friend remarked, "This is a small audience. I would have more confidence in the speaker if more people had come to hear him." Sighed the student, "Do you judge the value of a diamond by the number of people who look at it?"

590. An artist was painting a picture showing Columbus standing at a window gazing out to sea. A friend of the artist gasped as he glanced at the half-finished painting. "The scene includes a kind of

149

clock," observed the friend, "which was unknown during the days of Columbus." Gratefully, the artist removed the clock from the painting. We are equally wise when permitting good advice to remove errors from our life-scenes.

591. An awakened man is never recognized by society's masses. The human habit of professing a love for truth while really preferring fantasy is much too strong. An awakened man makes boots for people living in rocky country—but they insist on going barefoot.

592. A young brother and sister were seated in the front yard trying to play their new harmonicas. They tried to play a popular tune of the day but it resulted in more discord than music. A passing neighbor nodded in understanding of what was wrong. "You don't know the melody well enough to reproduce it," she informed. "You need advice from someone who knows a wrong note when he hears it." Truth-seekers also need help from that unique individual who knows a wrong psychic note when hearing it.

593. A nervous and insecure woman asked a teacher for help. He told her all about the great truths which can make everyone free. As he concluded she said, "Everything sounds so wonderfully right, but let me tell you why I hesitate. I fear that these new ideas may turn me into a nervous and insecure woman."

594. Remarked a student in a class in Tennessee, "We are so gullible when seeking guidance. If a teaching merely looks good and sounds good we foolishly assume it can help." The teacher nodded and replied, "The advertisement about a medicine never cured anyone."

595. It is obvious that few people know the difference between doing good for themselves and doing nothing for themselves. To deepen your insight into the difference, take paper and pencil. Entitle the first column *Doing Good* and the next column *Doing Nothing*. List examples under each heading. In the first column you might write *Eagerness to learn* and *Accepting each day as new*. The second column could include *Defending wrong thinking* and *Feeling threatened by truth*. See every addition as a messenger bearing helpful news.

596. A teacher nodded toward a typewriter in a corner of the classroom. He asked, "Can you have an intelligent relationship with that typewriter without knowing how it works?" The students shook their heads. "So," continued the teacher, "can you have an intelligent relationship with yourselves without knowing how you work?" Self-knowledge provides power with people and events.

597. A legend tells about an isolated area of the ocean crowded with abandoned and derelict ships. The vessels drift slowly about, bumping, disengaging, wandering, but remaining always within the lifeless waters. A distant observer of them might believe that important activities were taking place, but a closer watcher would know better. An awakened man knows that this is the condition of men and women on earth. And he knows that nothing real can happen until a ship has a captain.

598. Just as you open your home to friendly and honest people only, open your mind only to cordial and noble thoughts. What kind of mental home do you wish to live in? Your mind belongs to you and you alone,

so you can establish the pleasant conditions you wish your mind to have.

599. Two artists lived in the same city. One painted superb pictures of city life, while the other produced valueless paintings. Both then moved to the countryside. The excellent artist continued to create fine pictures, including scenes of hills and groves. The other man continued to produce inferior paintings of the surrounding scenes. One day he shouted excitedly, "I see the problem! I can never find surroundings worthy of my talents!"

600. A class in authentic esotericism heard, "Your usual friends approve of you by going along with your ways. An awakened man disapproves of you by not going along with your ways. Your one chance is to make a friend of an awakened man who knows enough to disapprove of you." The students signaled their understanding by smiling.

WHAT SELF-INSIGHT
WILL DO FOR YOU

601. Experiencing mental suffering is definitely not the same as passing through suffering. Here is where many make a mistake. We merely experience suffering when complaining about it at the same time that we have a peculiar enjoyment of it. We learn how to pass through anguish by studying its nature as it courses through us, just as a doctor examines physical illness. For example, see that suffering includes a feeling of being surrounded by enemies. Now realize that all enemies are banished through higher understanding.

602. Two women were leaving a home after a social gathering. One of them suddenly remembered she had left some of her possessions in the hall of the home. Her friend volunteered to get them, returning a moment later with some items—the wrong ones. The lesson is, never permit others to collect truth for you. Only you know what belongs to you.

603. A hiker walking alongside a river saw a child being carried downstream in a drifting boat. His rush toward the child attracted the attention of other people who joined and helped him. The child was soon rescued. Universal good thoughts rush to the aid of the individual who expresses one good thought.

604. Students in a class in Minnesota were asked to volunteer helpful ideas. One stated, "A person who does not play roles himself will never be deceived and hurt by the role-playing of others." A second student said, "One drop of your own sense is worth more than a library loaded with scholarly theories."

605. Healthy fruit can be given only by a healthy tree. Likewise, righteous judgment can be given only by a righteous mind. Right judgment can never be given by anyone who sees an evil which is an unconscious projection of his own evil. Nor can right judgment be delivered by anyone who appears virtuous by mere contrast with the other man's particular fault. A sober man who feels superior when viewing an alcoholic may be quite a cruel sober man.

606. The steps to self-discovery are as plain as the steps in your own home. To find yourself you must lose what you call yourself. To lose what you call yourself you must see how you consist of unconscious and

imaginary self-labels. To see how you consist of self-labels you must study yourself. To study yourself you must reach the point of willingness to lose what you call yourself.

607. "The way I go through my day can be described with a single sentence," stated an inquirer. "I feel vaguely uncomfortable." The teacher commented, "Of course you do. This is because there are so many things in your day that should not be there, like foxes in an orchard. Despair is one of the foxes. I will give you a clue for getting rid of it. Do not fear your own despair."

608. Feeling imprisoned by life is a hoax, but a hoax needing exposure. A French soldier was captured, placed in an unlocked dungeon, and told that any attempt to escape would be punished. But his cautious investigation revealed that his captors had departed, so he walked out a free man. You need not remain a captive of deceptive society.

609. A dissatisfied prince left the castle of his father the king to live as a warrior. He believed that combat would provide happiness. Finally seeing his error he returned to the barred entrance of the castle. Since his habit of fighting was still strong he tried to knock down the door, but it resisted. Changing his attitude, the prince quietly studied the barred door, which revealed a way to open it. Man's condition is similar. A turning point occurs when a wanderer no longer wants to fight, but wants to learn.

610. Anyone invited to the class of an authentic teacher must not enter with his usual beliefs and attitudes. They will not fit, any more than the wheels of a child's wagon will fit an automobile. Listeners

must not wish to promote or protect their own ideas, but must wish to rescue themselves.

611. A desire for sensational events prevents a correct investigation of life. A group of men and women met to discuss religion and philosophy. All agreed it would have been exciting to have witnessed the miracles reported in religious literature. What tragic delusion. Not one of them was capable of reflecting, "But how would the witnessing of a miracle change the kind of human being I am?"

612. Scientists tell us that the atmosphere surrounding the earth weighs trillions of tons. Yet it is not felt as a burden by us because of the correct nature of our physical bodies. Surrounding burdens of a psychic origin are not felt by whoever lives from his correct nature.

613. You need not anxiously wonder what to do. It is enough to not know what to do. Just quietly see that you do not know what to do and remain with that absence. The absence of conditioned and habitual thought frees the mind, permitting it to rise to fresh altitudes of observation and insight. A bird released from its cage to soar the skies is able to see everything below.

614. An unhappy man complained to a teacher, "People do not behave toward me as I desire." Instructed the teacher, "Never waste energy wondering why people do not behave as you wish. Instead, investigate why you think it necessary for them to behave as you wish." In this small lesson is great profit.

615. People are unaware of having noisy minds, therefore, they neglect to silence them. A noisy mind is one filled with defensive attitudes, aggressive

theories, unconscious anxieties. This mind cannot hear the messages of deliverance sent its way. Only a quiet mind that wants to learn can hear and absorb. The difference in the two conditions is similar to talking with someone in a noisy factory and talking with him in a peaceful park.

616. Results divide themselves into good and bad only if the person thinks from a mind that wrongly divides results into these opposites. By saying that one result is good he becomes the slave of its opposite which he calls bad. He divides like this in the belief that his individuality is invested in what he calls good, but this individuality is merely a collection of self-labels. Understand just this much for now. It will come as your first glimpse of home after a long and weary journey.

617. Anyone falling into a crisis yearns for release from tension. One great release occurs when he is told, "It's not your fault." Cosmic insight supplies authentic release. When in trouble of any kind do not believe that you are connected permanently with the faulty self that is always in trouble. There is no such permanent connection, any more than a ship is connected with dangerous icebergs presently surrounding it. The ship can sail to a clear sea. So can you. What release!

618. A woman in a study group said to the teacher, "We are seeing the necessity of ending self-delusion. We will take any shocking information you supply if only it will help eliminate this harmful habit." The teacher supplied, "Watch someone carefully when he hints at how much he cares for others. The fact is, he does not care at all, but only wants to be *known* as someone who cares. Anyone able to face this fact in himself will make it out of the dungeon."

619. Thinking from unconsciously borrowed ideas is like building your home from plans provided by a man whose house has just collapsed. Your mind is capable of an astonishing variety of original thoughts which serve individual needs. Think from your own mind.

620. A scientist invented a marvelous soap which could clean anything instantly. But he was shocked at how few people really wanted it. One day he was walking down the street in his perfectly clean clothes when he was stopped by an excited stranger. It was obvious that the stranger's clothes had not been washed in years. Holding up a small magazine, the stranger cried out to the scientist, "Friend, let me tell you about a marvelous soap I have invented through heavenly revelation. Let me explain how it will save you from everything unclean."

HOW A NEW STUDENT WAS HELPED

621. A new student wanted to know, "Why is the world the way it is?" The teacher replied, "I will tell you, but I want your own observation of the social scene to confirm the answer. A man deluded into thinking he has saved himself will compulsively try to save others, which is one reason why the world is the way it is."

622. Friendship with fantasy is the friendship of a duck with a fox. And unawareness of the friendship does not prevent the damage done by the fantasy. So a vexed man should ask himself, "Why do I experience so much destruction? Maybe I am in fact living in friendship with fantasy without realizing it. I will investigate."

623. During a class session the topic of stimulating experiences came up. The teacher informed, "People

confuse stimulating experiences with instructive experiences. Mere stimulation teaches nothing, in fact, it deepens delusion. An instructive experience is any experience in which you prove to yourself that you did not know as much as you assumed you knew. Take that as a guide and you will never go wrong."

624. Imagine yourself watching a man sitting in a chair who is under the spell of hypnosis. As an observer, you know he is hypnotized, but he is unaware of his state. This is how Truth sees humanity. Truth sees man as hypnotized and unaware, but with an opportunity to awaken. Seize your opportunity by using this book.

625. "I talk to myself endlessly," someone stated, "which does nothing for me. What can be done about it?" Replied the instructor, "It is a common condition. Because of psychic hypnosis you are dominated by mechanical forces—mechanical thoughts, feelings, desires, imaginations. Fortunately, you are now learning to replace mechanicalness with liberty from all such whirlpools."

626. A map of Europe was once printed in which Switzerland was omitted completely. Those glancing at the faulty map sensed that something was missing, which aroused an urge to learn what was wrong. A close look at our lives reveals that self-awareness is missing, which arouses energy for inner correction.

627. It was graduation day at a school for demons. The principal demon congratulated the graduating demons and handed out diplomas. He then gave a brief speech, saying, "This class has but one task, but it is of overwhelming importance in keeping stupid human beings as stupid as they are. Your task is to make evil

look like good and to make good look like evil."
Needless to say, the demons achieved great success
throughout the world. But that is not surprising, for after
all they received full cooperation from human beings.

628. There is small profit in talking with those who
do not know that they do not know. A caller told a real
teacher, "I am considered to be a scholar, an intellectual and a philosopher. So what lofty subject shall we
discuss?" Sighing slightly, the teacher remarked, "How
about apple pie?"

629. A teacher ended his talk and left the room. His
assistant stood up and faced the audience. "You have
just heard the liberating truth," he stated, "so the
decision is now yours. Choose in favor of yourself.
I will add one other point. If you can look up and
down at the same time, you can also have your way
and the cosmic way at the same time."

630. A story from India tells of a wanderer who
habitually picked up shiny stones wherever he saw them,
which he placed into a sack on his back. One night he
fell into a well. His cry for help brought a rescuer who
threw a rope down the well. But three times the rope
broke. Finally, the wanderer had sense enough to
remove the heavy sack of shiny but useless stones. He
was hauled to safety. The dropping of shiny but
useless ideas is necessary for self-rescue. Drop the idea
that you must fear other people.

631. Suppose you hand someone a book containing
a great scientific secret for turning stones into sapphires.
And suppose he responds with displeasure, "But *must*
I do it? I prefer doing something more interesting." A
strange reply? Yet this is the same kind of strange

reply made by people when offered the great cosmic secret for turning their lives from defeat to victory.

632. An illuminated man noticed how many of his disciples unwisely worshipped human personality instead of valuing truth itself. He wished to correct this. One morning a disciple said, "Is it not right to praise you? After all, you have a great reputation for spirituality." Replied the teacher, "Let my reputation make you personally happy."

633. Self-repair must be one's first order of business, otherwise he is like a seaman too worried about the leaks in his boat to sail forward. Self-repair proceeds rapidly when one constantly questions his present life. Among other things this means that physical or financial security must not be taken as psychological security. Safe and wealthy men tremble.

634. We can call a deer a horse but it will still not have the power of a horse. What a man calls strength is really weakness. It is weakness in the form of misunderstanding. Man thinks he has strength to make himself and others happy, but this is merely a form of vanity. The only strength capable of making anyone happy is the power of his Cosmic Mind, not his self-centered and petty mind.

635. Said a member of a group in Kentucky, "Over the years this class has given me just the right idea at the right time. At one time I felt like a jar into which everyone poured their troubles. A lesson here revealed how my own false need for these people attracted them and their troubles. That helped me to keep my time and energy for my own real needs."

636. Nothing harmful can ever happen to you as a result of dropping habitual ideas about yourself. This includes the idea that you must be appreciated or socially successful or should be married or should get a raise in pay. It may appear harmful at first, but that wrong feeling passes, leaving you with true satisfaction. It is like dropping an old and uncomfortable coat to discover that the weather never called for it in the first place.

637. Most people live in a lonely land, visited only by a variety of storms. If this describes your location I will tell you something interesting. This location is yours only because you do not as yet know about the alternative. In this book we are traveling together toward the Other Land.

638. A young woman was shopping for shoes. She was so attracted to a certain pair of shoes she overlooked the fact that they did not fit properly, a fact observed by the shoe salesman. Wishing to help, the salesman asked the young woman to stand up in the shoes, which made them even more uncomfortable. The salesman then asked, "Is that what you really want?" The understanding young woman did not buy the shoes. If your life looks attractive but feels uncomfortable, ask yourself, "Is that what you really want?" This awakens higher understanding.

639. See deeper into people. It is essential to your own awakening. See their real motives, their actual attitudes. It is quite simple. Imagine yourself in a roomful of chattering people, smiling and waving. Study their faces carefully. What do you see? You see a roomful of scared human beings doing their best to play their nervous roles. You don't want to live like that.

640. Three inquirers were given a project in self-questioning. One man was to ask himself, "How do you expect to change yourself without studying yourself?" Another was instructed to inquire, "Why do you cling to the precarious perch of your habitual assumptions?" A woman was to ask herself, "When will you place self-insight before self-defense?"

WHY WATCHFULNESS IS WISE

641. Man's carelessness toward his own life is like a child who plays daily in a cleared field. Small weeds appear, but he is so wrapped up in his play he fails to notice them. Later, the weeds grow thick enough to restrict his play and annoy his mind. Still, he does nothing to remove them. Later yet, when play becomes impossible, what does he do?   He blames the weeds!

642. A member of a group commented, "Just when you think society has recovered its sanity it does some stupid thing that proves otherwise. This fact turned me toward inner investigation more than anything else. I finally had to face the blunt fact that there is absolutely no help out there."

643. Part of a person knows he is handling life all wrong, but that single part is surrounded by dozens of wrong parts. It is like a class in public school. One sincere student wishes to learn, but his indifferent classmates cause a commotion by shouting and tossing objects. Our work consists of teaching the earnest inner student while ignoring the disinterested ones. Dwell upon this illustration.

644. Out of foolish sentimentality a businessman protected a stranger accused of damaging some

property. The businessman then discovered that his own property had been damaged by the stranger. People rarely see that the positions they protect so fiercely are the very positions which damage their lives. It is the dawning of a totally new kind of intelligence to see this.

645. A good shepherd tried to lead his flock from a barren land to green meadows. The sheep resisted with the stubborn belief, "There is no land but this." People decline to move away from their wretchedness for fear there may not be another place for them. There is. And that new place is a happy place.

646. As an interesting mental exercise, see that a person rejects a fact which does not agree with what he already believes. Now see something else. See that his rejection of the fact keeps him in psychic prison. See even more. See that a fact-rejecting person can help himself by seeing a fact as a key to liberty, not as an enemy. Exercise in this way frequently. Start with an idea and add other right ideas to it. This builds logic, just as you might build a solid wall with one brick at a time.

647. "When first attending these classes," testified a student, "I wondered why so much attention was given to human fear. Now I see the wisdom in it. Man is like a fugitive who has run so long and so hard he has forgotten what he fears. We investigate fear in order to understand and dissolve it."

648. An unhealed psychic wound is one that has not been disconnected from a false self-identity. We prevent healing by repeating *"My* defeat" or *"I* am hurt." For an immediate cure, disconnect the imaginary self from the past experience. What happens to physical discomfort

when you disconnect the physical body from a blazing sun? The discomfort vanishes. It is like that.

649. A beginner on the path should realize a certain fact about himself. He should see how his interest in self-newness is high one moment but may be snatched away the next moment by a dazzling trifle. Awareness of this should not be a cause for dismay, but should be taken as another helpful lesson about one's actual inconsistency. Awareness of lack precedes the ending of lack. Absence of food in the refrigerator arouses interest in obtaining food.

650. No longer give your attention to things that cannot happen, instead, give attention to what can actually happen to you. Do you wish to find security outside of your own illuminated nature? It cannot happen. Do you wish freedom from feeling trapped by other people? It can happen, for wrong thoughts alone cause that feeling. By doing this you give your attention to a treasure map, not to a book of fiction.

651. A man was captured by some outlaws and tied to a tree each night. One night a storm struck. Assuming the prisoner would not try to escape in such fierce weather, the outlaws relaxed their guard. But that was the precise night the prisoner made a successful effort to escape. I will tell you something worth more than all the gold in the world. The best time to double your effort toward psychic escape is when everything seems to conspire against you. Surprise the psychic captors with a sudden burst of energy such as refusing falseness.

652. Said a student in class, "I am convinced that a study of human insincerity is essential to our plans for self-rescue." A second student requested, "Give us

an example of what you mean by insincerity." Replied the first student, "People smilingly assure you they want the truth but when truth approaches whatever they are hiding you see their faces change."

653. The task of a factory employee was to inspect the complicated machinery. It was difficult and tiring work. One day he was told, "You need not do this any more. Scientific instruments will do the work." With great relief the employee turned to his new assignment. It is a great day when one realizes that he can discontinue his tiring psychic tasks. He does not need to be impressive or desirable; he can relax and be himself.

654. Realization is immediate and right action. A passenger realizing he is on the wrong bus takes immediate and right action. He gets off the wrong bus and boards the right one. Do you wish to take immediate and right action about anything? Obtain realization. Then, problems with love and sex will disappear.

655. Suppose you wish to build a home, but have no knowledge of necessary procedures. Then you meet an expert who freely supplies his knowledge and time. He shows you how to start, where to obtain materials and so on. So with his patient guidance you construct a safe and comfortable home. That is a simple illustration of how an awakened man helps those who request help in building a cosmic residence. But remember, only those who realize they are homeless can make a sincere request for help.

656. Said a teacher to a group of inquirers, "Are you afraid of other people—and tired of it? Are you trying

to prove things about yourself—and exhausted by the futile attempts? Are you anxious over tomorrow—and weary of living with that anxiety? If you are tired enough I can teach you something. Return tomorrow and we will start."

657. People assume that beliefs can open the highway to happiness, when in fact a man's beliefs keep him on endless detours. The reason beliefs cannot sustain anyone is because life's events do not believe in beliefs.

658. A story was told about an ancient hero who was determined to rescue the king's jewels which were guarded by a dragon in a cavern. Each day for many days the hero descended into the cavern to battle the dragon and take whatever jewels he could until all were recovered. By descending bravely into ourselves we recover our cosmic jewels. One cosmic jewel is confidence when handling others.

659. Man's ignorance prevents him from seeing his absurd reasoning. It is like the man who brought a board to an artist with the request, "Draw a life-size picture of George Washington on this board." The artist told him that the board was too short. Replied the man, "Then paint it by letting Washington's legs hang down over the end of the board."

660. As part of a group discussion, one member asked another, "What difficulty did you face when first coming to class?" The other member replied, "It was hard for me to admit that my life was out of control and always had been. I was helped enormously by hearing that self-honesty is power for self-newness."

YOU CAN CONSTRUCT A NEW LIFE

661. A change in exterior conditions does not change human nature. Suppose an old and creaky house is torn down. Some carpenters use its aged lumber to build another house with a different shape. The shape is different but the house is still old. Know for sure that only new facts can construct a new life. New facts are available. Find them. You will be glad you did.

662. Never feel downhearted if progress seems dreadfully slow, if nothing seems to change. Dismay is simply another wrong reaction of the mind. This useless reaction can be stopped. Remember that. You may face ten thousand locked doors, but the key you are now acquiring will open every one of them.

663. Anyone can learn to drop a feeling of sorrow or frustration the moment he sees it within himself, but it takes practice. You must first be aware that you have the feeling, which is not the same thing as simply feeling it. You must stand as an outside observer of the feeling. This independent observer is the very power itself for dropping the sorrow, just as you drop a hot pan when aware of its discomfort.

664. "Society may not be perfect," said a visitor to a class, "but surely it can teach us how to live with maximum happiness." Answered the teacher, "The only thing society teaches us is how to be scared. Now, will you listen to that same society when it tells you how to stop being scared? You might as well listen to a goat teaching you to fly."

665. Ask yourself the plain question, "Why does man fail to reach the other shore where real contentment

resides?" The answer is, he tries to cross a bridge existing only in his imagination. It is pure imagination that society's schemes can build a bridge. Only individual self-renewal can succeed. Think about this.

666. The value of a study group is illustrated by a story from Asia. A man lived in a pleasant village located in a secret valley in the Himalayas. One day he wandered so far down a mountain trail he could not find his way back home. After many years of rueful roaming he found himself passing a camp alongside a river. His head jerked around as he heard familiar music. Investigating, he met other lost citizens of the pleasant village. They invited him to join their plans for finding the way back home. He accepted enthusiastically.

667. A schoolteacher sat at her desk quietly observing her young pupils. She could already see that Bobby would develop into a mild-mannered adult, burning with suppressed hostility. And obviously, Helen was on her way to a ruthless pursuit of her desires, destroying herself as she went along. The teacher knew that only one thing could prevent the tragic downhill slide of all her pupils—contact with the shocking but saving Truth.

668. "Those with the most confidence about transforming the world are those with the least confidence about transforming themselves." Do you know who said that? It was said by a man who was trying to transform the world because he had no confidence in transforming himself.

669. As an assignment a truth-class was given a question to think about and to discuss at the next meeting. The question was, "Can you see that cooperation with cosmic truth is the same as cooperation with your real nature?" Discuss this interesting question with yourself. The answer is delightful.

670. Truth alone makes sense to the sensible person. A dozen men were sent alone into different parts of a vast wilderness to test their ability to survive. Each was given the same equipment and identical instructions. Those who came out best in the test were those who followed the instructions the most carefully. One of them reported, "I saw how the instructions made perfect sense, how they matched with my own feelings of survival."

671. Build your life as a Bavarian king once built his castle. The king wished to make his castle as independent as possible, so wells, vegetable gardens and other necessities were established inside the walls. Be sufficient for yourself. Live from your own resources of wisdom and strength. Make your mind your independent castle. Now, other people cannot invade and plunder your life.

672. Someone remarked, "I feel as if I belong to others but never to myself. What can I do about it?" Asked the teacher, "How strong is your wish to belong to yourself? Make it mighty enough to conquer your own resistances. That is a fine start."

673. It is not a fall that bothers us so much as the knowledge that others have witnessed our fall. Then in our embarrassment we explain and justify and accuse, which reveals our slavery to the opinions of others toward us. This proves that human beings are much more interested in presenting a good appearance than in correcting the cause of a fall. That is as ridiculous as placing a fancy carpet over a broken floor instead of making necessary repairs. No wonder we fall so often!

674. An alert mind can learn a thousand things about other people by seeing through their remarks. Take

someone who repeatedly informs you of how busy he is. He is trying to convince himself that his empty life is full and important. Or take anyone who evades any questioning of his motives. The harder a bird tries to draw you away from its nest the more it gives away its secret.

675. Reported a member of a class, "In reading esoteric books I have run repeatedly into a certain teaching. It says we can have one thing or another, but we can't have both. I can have my insistence that I already know the answers to life or I can really have the answers, but I can't have both. That has value in helping us to choose rightly."

676. A preferred idea is not necessarily a self-uplifting idea. How many people understand—really understand—this simple fact? Few. Preference arises from a nervous need to promote or protect oneself. An unburdened mind has no such need. Experiment at dropping acquired and preferred ideas. It is like dropping unwanted boxes of bricks.

677. It is obvious that most people live under the dictatorship of accidental influences. The course of their day is set by unexpected news, unfamiliar conditions, unpleasant behavior by others. Almost anything on the outside dictates their moods on the inside. But just as music is not under the influence of darkness, those who possess cosmic power are not under accidental influences of the exterior world. They live from themselves.

678. A father was teaching his young son the art of making special kinds of wooden whistles. One time when the father was absent from home he received a letter of discouragement from his puzzled son. The father

replied with several helpful suggestions, then concluded, "If you really want to understand, you will really understand." And so will we.

679. A hungry wanderer met the owner of a fruit orchard. The orchardist generously gave the wanderer fifteen minutes to pick all the fruit he wanted. Forgetting everything else the wanderer swiftly filled his sacks with fruit. Spiritually hungry people must forget the trivial affairs of life to make the most of their present opportunity for self-fulfillment.

680. About to take a trip, a teacher gave instructions to his assistants at the esoteric school. "When talking with newcomers," said the teacher, "remember a sad fact about human nature. Give a person the slightest opportunity to feel sorry for himself and he will do it. So never say anything that encourages self-pity, for instance, never agree when someone tells you how badly he has been treated by others. Instead, teach people to be brave and honest; show them how to drop yesterday in order to find themselves today."

LET COSMIC FACTS
CARRY YOU FORWARD

681. In a scene on television a man opened a door to find himself staring at a solid brick wall. The door went nowhere. This is like human plans which do not take cosmic principles into account. Everything changes when they are taken into account. We go somewhere.

682. One sign of a mind that works against itself is the need to blame others for one's troubles. It is impossible for such a divided mind to be content,

171

even if exterior circumstances are favorable. Trying to be happy while in mental contradiction is as futile as trying to grab a handful of air. Contentment resides in mental unity.

683. Said a teacher to his class, "I wish you to write down and memorize a single sentence about spiritual advice. Here it is. Any advice which does not aim at making you a new kind of person internally is utterly worthless. I will repeat with emphasis. *Any advice which does not aim at making you a new kind of person internally is utterly worthless.*"

684. Make an experiment. Watch what happens when you ask someone a simple question. In many cases the question could be answered yes or no, but do you receive such a brief reply? Rarely. Give someone the slightest opportunity to make a speech and he makes a speech. This experiment makes you more aware of human compulsion and nervousness, which helps your own stability. A golfer noticing the wrong move of another player does not make the same mistake himself.

685. If you want peaches you must not visit a lemon grove. If you want self-command you must not live by principles that prevent self-command. If you want peace of mind you must not accept beliefs that block peace of mind. If you want peaches, visit a peach orchard.

686. Some students heard, "You are not really afraid of next week or next year. You are in fear of yourself. You are afraid because you know very well that you are unreal, and therefore know also that this fictitious self cannot handle the future or anything else. Be real, for then the entire problem of the future will disappear

in the light of Now. There are no calendars in the celestial kingdom."

687. Those wishing real success must stop listening to whatever does not contribute to it. Flattery is an example of wrong listening. Flattery is simply telling a man the wonderful things he already believes about himself. If a pine tree can produce apples, we win what is right by listening to what is wrong.

688. Man lives like a prisoner in court about to be pronounced guilty. Failing to understand himself he agrees with the verdict by adding self-condemnation. But guilt is a false reaction because it perpetuates the illusion that an individual self exists which should feel guilty. The man falsely comforts himself, "I may be guilty but at least I exist as a guilty individual." Above the error of feeling guilty is a right response. It consists of consciousness of self-defeating behavior. This ends self-defeat.

689. A class was told, "A person's level of psychic maturity can be judged by what impresses him. Is he impressed by goodness or by glamour? Is he impressed by private integrity or by a public appearance of respectability? I will give you something to think about. A respectable institution is simply a small delusion that has grown into a large delusion."

690. Are most human beings reasonably logical? Far from it. Tell someone, "The reason you fall into traps along the trail is because you insist upon hiking that particular trail." Will he make an effort to comprehend? No. He will continue to fall into traps until his pain compels him to ask why he illogically follows the trail having all those traps.

691. Weariness provides opportunity. Alertness seizes opportunity. These two sentences describe the entire method for spiritual rebirth. So be weary with the unworkable. Be alert toward the truly practical. You will make progress like a traveler on a dry prairie who first sights a single tree, then a green grove, then a pleasant forest.

692. Suppose you set a glass of water before someone who then requests, "May I have a glass of water?" That illustrates what happens when spiritually thirsty people are given what they request. Because of psychic hypnosis they are unable to see what is plainly set before them. The development of cosmic sight must be a chief aim. Power and pleasure will be a chief result.

693. A teacher instructed, "You must study false happiness. The happiness of this smiling man or that active woman is pure illusion. It is a pathetic substitute for the quietness of being one with oneself. Such a person presents a happy exterior because he has temporarily succeeded in suppressing his gnawing doubts about himself. There is no need to live like that, so don't."

694. Self-punishment has no place whatever in our task of becoming whole. Do you know people who enjoy their sourness so much they would fight anyone who tried to give them happiness? They are good examples of self-punishing people. One student of higher truth gradually released secret sourness by realizing deeply that he was in fact his own punishment.

695. Do not be like a man who lights a lamp in a dark cavern and then closes his eyes. This is what we do when refusing to face an obvious fact. An observed

fact is the very light that guides us out of the cavern. Observe this fact: Innocence is true power.

696. A teacher entered the hall and spoke to a new class. "Understand human nature and you understand the cause of all problems on earth. Understand cosmic nature and you understand the cure for all problems on earth. So we will explore both human nature and cosmic nature. The collected information will be both surprising and constructive. The student who endures will know what it means to no longer be an enemy to himself." After pausing the teacher asked, "Do you really wish to take the journey? If so, we can proceed." The students nodded.

697. A story was written about an early settler in Australia who established a sheep ranch. When asked by other settlers to take time out for social affairs he answered politely, "That is not my purpose in being here." His ranch prospered. Give that same answer when anyone tries to distract you from the inner task. You will prosper in dealing with others, for self-success guarantees other-success.

698. Be aware of subtle suggestions of fear and defeat offered to you by fearful and defeated people, then ignore them. Nothing in your authentic nature needs to listen to such unhealthy suggestions. As if a talented tenor listens to traffic noise!

699. Several students brought their difficulties to their instructor. One said he was discouraged, another admitted he had suppressed hostility, and so on. The teacher replied cheerfully, "Discouragement? What has that to do with it? Proceed. Hostility? What has that to do with it? Proceed."

700. A sea captain anchored his ship a mile offshore of a paradise island, believing the natives were hostile. Later he learned that the island's king had been waving palm branches as messages of welcome. You need not wait for an invitation to enter the royal estate. You are already invited. The royal estate is yours the moment you accept it. Think what this means. No more waiting! So accept it now.

SEE SPECIAL OFFER
ON NEXT PAGE

"Vernon Howard helps me focus on what really matters, not what scatters."

SPECIAL OFFER

FREE booklets • FREE shipping

For each item you order from the list below (#1 - #5), select one FREE booklet of your choice (A - F):

1. **Mystic Path to Cosmic Power** .... *(New edition)* $12
2. **Your Power of Natural Knowing** .... *(Book)* .... $ 9
3. **Solved—The Mystery of Life** .... *(Book)* $10
4. **The Power of Esoterics** .... *(NEW book)* $12
5. **The Laws of Spiritual Development** *(3-Cassette Album)* $20

Choose a FREE booklet with each above item ordered:

   A. *50 Ways to See Thru People*   *(Booklet)*
   B. *Conquer Harmful Anger 100 Ways*   *(Booklet)*
   C. *Your Power to Say NO*   *(Booklet)*
   D. *Live Above this Crazy World*   *(Booklet)*
   E. *Practical Exercises for Inner Harmony* *(Booklet)*
   F. *50 Ways to Get Help from God*   *(Booklet)*

━ ━ ━ ━ ━ ━ ━ ━ ORDER FORM ━ ━ ━ ━ ━ ━ ━ ━

For ordering: **See address on opposite page**

ITEM	PRICE	QTY	FREE BKLT	TOTAL
1. Mystic Path to Cosmic Power	$12			
2. Your Power of Natural Knowing	$ 9			
3. Solved—The Mystery of Life	$10			
4. The Power of Esoterics *(New!)*	$12			
5. The Laws of Spiritual Development	$20			
				$

Name _____

Address_____

City_____ State_____Zip _____

XGNL

178

ABOUT
NEW LIFE FOUNDATION
****

New Life is a nonprofit organization founded by Vernon Howard in the 1970's for the distribution and dissemination of his teachings. It is for anyone who has run out of his own answers and has said to himself, "There has to be something else." These teachings *are* the something else. All are encouraged to explore and apply these profound truths—*they work!*

The Foundation conducts classes on a regular basis throughout Arizona, Colorado and Southern California. They are an island of sanity in a confused world. The atmosphere is friendly, light and uplifting. Don't miss the opportunity to attend your first New Life class.

For details on books, tapes and classes write:

Headquarters
NEW LIFE FOUNDATION
PO Box 2230
Pine, Arizona 85544
(520) 476-3224

Web: www.anewlife.org
E-mail: info@anewlife.org
Vernon Howard, Founder

TELL A FRIEND!
SEND US NAMES

NOTES

NOTES

NOTES

NOTES

NOTES

NOTES

NOTES

NOTES

NOTES

NOTES

NOTES

NOTES

NOTES